the LONDON of

SHERLOCK HOLMES

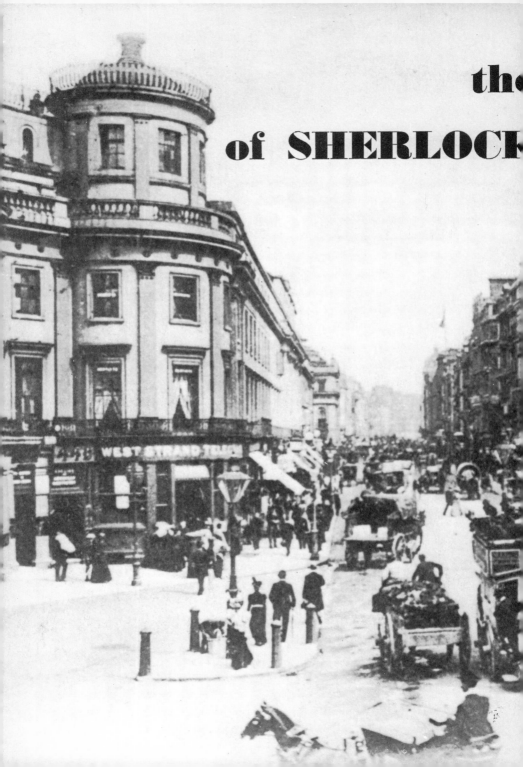

the
of SHERLOCK

LONDON
HOLMES

Michael Harrison

DRAKE PUBLISHERS INC NEW YORK

To

HENRY EMBERSON

Free Vintner

for many a pleasantly
meditative hour over the
pleasantly meditative wine . . .

'Costly the vintage as thy purse can buy,
But not expressed in fancy; rich, not gaudy . . .'

ISBN 87749-223-9

Published in 1972 by
Drake Publishers Inc
381 Park Avenue South
New York, N.Y. 10016

Printed in Great Britain

CONTENTS

LIST OF ILLUSTRATIONS

7

8

10

CHAPTER 1

Mr Holmes Comes to Town

It was in July 1877 or 1878—the exact year cannot now be established with accuracy—that young Mr Sherlock Holmes came down from his university, and, in his own words, 'took rooms in Montague Street, just round the corner from the British Museum'.

The 'rooms', as my own research has proved, were at No 24, Montague Street, Russell Square, a still-standing four-storey house of severely late-Georgian aspect which was incorporated into the Lonsdale Hotel some seventy years ago. In 1875, Mrs Holmes took a seven-year lease on No 24, entering into possession of the eminently respectable house at Michaelmas (29 September) of that same year. It would be stretching coincidence too far to assume that Mrs Holmes was not related in some way to young Mr Holmes, and we may assume that the lady took the house in Montague Street to provide a home for Sherlock when he should come down from the university and begin his professional career in London.

No 'headquarters' could have been more convenient for Sherlock Holmes. As he said, the British Museum, on which one looked from the front windows of No 24, had its imposing main entrance 'just round the corner'. Around the other corner, just a few yards along Great Russell Street, going east, were the offices of the Pharmaceutical Society, recently altered internally, but outwardly looking much as it did when twenty-three-year-old Sherlock consulted the books in its extensive library to acquire that knowledge which was to make him one of the world's greatest experts on toxicology, notably in its relation to crime. Even as early as 1881,

Sidney Paget's sketch of Sherlock Holmes, made about 1891 when Holmes
was thirty-seven

the year in which Holmes and his future Boswell, John H. Watson,
MD, met, Watson notes that Holmes is 'well up in belladonna,
opium, and poisons generally'.

Bloomsbury Square, at the north-west corner of which the painted
stucco offices of the Pharmaceutical Society stand, has been completely rebuilt on the east side, the entire width being filled by the
towering neo-Classic headquarters of the Liverpool Victoria Building Society. The construction of an underground car-park beneath
the gardens of the square has thinned out the trees, for which some
crude 'service' buildings in a particularly nasty shade of purple
brick seem an unacceptable substitute. But the buildings on the west
side of the square, though having been refronted several times, are

The British Museum as it was at the end of the last century, and as it still remains. The balconied house at the extreme upper right-hand corner of the photograph is at the end of Montague Street

almost all contemporary with the laying out of this, London's oldest square, now nearly 350 years old.

To the south of the square, linking Bloomsbury Way (Hart Street, Bloomsbury, in Holmes's day) with High Holborn, is still unaltered Southampton Place (Southampton Street in 1877), in which, at No 6, might be seen a brightly-polished brass plate, bearing the legend :

JOHN WATSON, M.D.

Again, it can hardly be coincidence that when 'young Stamford' —Watson calls him 'my dresser at Bart's'—wishes to introduce Watson to Holmes, Watson lunches first at the Holborn Restaurant, since 'the Holborn'—popular from the start with the Prince of Wales (later King Edward VII) and his fellow Freemasons—was the nearest first-class restaurant to Watson's consulting rooms in just-across-the-street No 6.

The Holborn Restaurant, with its shabby but still impressive dining-rooms, Masonic temples and airy entrance hall and lofty corridors, was demolished some years back, a modern but not altogether ugly office building going up on its site. However, the National Westminster Bank next door occupies a building nearly contemporary with the old 'Holborn', and the famous silver shop at the corner of nearby Parker Street is unaltered since the day when Watson crossed Holborn to his consulting rooms.

If, as seems likely from the numerous mentions of strong drink in the Canon, neither Holmes nor Watson was abstemious in the matter of liquor, Watson may well have slipped across Holborn to 'have a quick one' at 'The Princess Louise'. This magnificent pub, named after the artist daughter of Queen Victoria (Louise married the Marquess of Lorne, eldest son of the 8th Duke of Argyll, in 1871) has suffered less than most at the hands of redecorating vandals: it is well worth a visit if only for a sight of its lavish tiling, an art which, fortunately, seems to be reviving amongst British ceramic manufacturers. I remember the 'Louise's' most popular pre-

The Medical School, University of London, Gower Street. It was here, in 1878, that John H. Watson took his degree of Doctor of Medicine, as he relates in ' A Study in Scarlet '

World War II lunch: a huge dinner-plate slopping over with bub-
bling Welsh rarebit (6d) and a half-pint of bitter beer (4½d)—total
cost, with a repletion which never halted this side of agonising
dyspepsia, a mere 10½d, or in today's money, 4½p.

Just as Holmes's 'rooms' in Montague Street were wonderfully
convenient for him, so were the rooms—perhaps the whole house
(the *London Post Office Directory* for 1878 seems to say as much)
—at No 6, Southampton Street (now Place) wonderfully convenient
for Watson.

In June 1878, Watson had taken his degree of MD at the
University of London medical school in Gower Street, a few
minutes' walk from Southampton Street. However, the MD is a
'final' qualification, and with the lesser qualifications which usually
precede it—membership of the Royal College of Surgeons and
a licence from the Royal College of Physicians—Watson would have
been sufficiently qualified to be able to set up his plate and go into
medical practice.

Perhaps a year or two older than Holmes, Watson had his sights
set on a military career, but intended to qualify himself as fully as
possible before entering the Army Medical Service (now the Royal
Army Medical Corps). In 1878 the Army Medical Service was only
'para-military', staffed with what were, in effect, uniformed civilian
medical men under the generally not-very-strict control of the
Surgeon-General (who, some twenty years before Watson had taken
his MD, had turned out to have been a *woman*!).

The abolition of commissions by purchase in 1871 had not, by
1878, had the intended effect of 'democratising' the Army and, old
snobberies dying hard, the standing of the medical man in the Army
was both ambiguous and, too often, 'unacceptable' to snobbish
holders of Her Majesty's commission. On the other hand, a Doctor
of Medicine was recognised throughout the caste-conscious ranks of
Victorian society as having established himself *professionally*, as
having gained the status of 'gentleman'. Watson seems either to
have been a prudent planner or the recipient of excellent advice in
having decided thus to defend himself against snobs in the mess.
The faithful Watson records that Holmes had no great opinion of
his flat-mate's intelligence, but the careful planning evident in
Watson's entry into a military career tells us quite another story.
Though he never refers to himself as a Scotsman, Watson is a well-

known Scots name, and certainly in his calculation of the best way of entering the Army Medical Service he demonstrates a truly Scots canniness.

The latter part of 1878 Watson spent in learning the essentially military part of his work. The prescribed course for Army surgeons was taken, in those days, at Netley Hospital, Hampshire, to which it would have been quite possible to 'commute' from London. The Netley trains ran from Waterloo Station, a mere quarter-hour's walk down Little Queen Street (widened and straightened after 1903 into the present Kingsway), across a narrower Strand than ours and over Rennie's Waterloo Bridge to the station.

In any case, the *Post Office London Directory* shows that Watson —if it *is* our John Watson, MD—kept his plate at No 6, Southampton Street, Bloomsbury Square, for several years after 1878.

Waterloo Station was extensively, and magnificently, reconstructed after World War I, the architecture being influenced by the fact that the London and South Western Railway Company's directors wished to make it, in addition to a modernised railway terminus, a memorial to those of the railway's servants who had fought and died in the recent war. However, there is still quite a lot of the old plank-built Waterloo of the time at which Watson was commuting to Netley; and those who wish to see what sort of a station it was from which the young Army doctor caught his train to Hampshire can find the remains of old Waterloo Station in the part nearest to Waterloo Road.

The Waterloo district by the Thames has undergone radical changes over the past quarter-century: the gaunt concrete bulks of the Royal Festival Hall, the Queen Elizabeth Hall and the National Theatre rising from where—it hardly seems yesterday—a huddle of sooty, late-Georgian, two-storey cottages, with an occasional Georgian mansion in its sadly restricted grass plot, maintained a defiant outpost of domesticity amongst the wharves and builders' yards over which ran, and still runs, the arch-borne railway viaduct. But even now, at the back of all the concrete modernity of two concert halls and a theatre, there still exist survivals of the old Waterloo: the dingy splendour of early nineteenth century Stamford Street; rows of cottages which cower under the arches of the thundering viaduct; costers' stalls in nearby Lambeth Walk and the Cut—filling up now with chain-stores and chromium, but still hold-

In 1878, Holmes was living, to use his own phrase, ' in rooms in Montague Street, just round the corner from the British Museum.' At No 24, a Mrs Holmes lived from 1877 to 1883. It is the right-hand house of the pair now forming the Lonsdale Hotel

ing out as always diminishing enclaves of the independent spirit—the spirit which made Holmes reject the choice of some established profession and risk his future in one of his own creation: that of the world's first 'consulting detective'.

It seems odd that Holmes, living in Montague Street, and Watson, attending lectures at the University of London Medical School—a few hundred yards only separated Montague Street from Gower Street—did not meet until 'young Stamford' introduced them at St Bartholomew's Hospital—Bart's to all who work there or know it well—in January 1881.

But so it was. Even though both Watson and Holmes must have used the same streets, the same cosy Victorian bars, attended the same vigorous Victorian music halls—especially the Oxford, at St Giles' Circus, which, only five minutes' walk along Great Russell street from Montague Street, *must* have been visited by Holmes. It was not all knock-about comic stuff at the Oxford; the big stars of the Victorian music-hall were proud to appear at the Oxford, and it remained a top-billing hall until, after World War I, it was pulled down to make way for the Lyons' Oxford Street Corner House, now itself turned over to other purposes.

One survival from Holmes's day still stands at the corner of Great Russell Street and Tottenham Court Road: the 'Horseshoe', once a great hotel with a multiplicity of bars. It is no longer an hotel, but the bars remain. The interior has been completely deprived of its original Victorian character, but the exterior, with its typical decorative ironwork of the 1870s, more than merely hints at the more spacious London of Holmes's younger days.

In November 1878 Watson, having completed his military surgeon's course at Netley, was attached to the 5th Northumberland Fusiliers as an assistant-surgeon, and set sail for India just as the second Afghan War broke out. Eight months later he was to find himself at the disastrous Battle of Maiwand, fought on 27 July 1880. Watson was to reflect later that he got off lightly with no greater injury than being struck on the shoulder by a Jezail bullet, 'which shattered the bone and grazed the sub-clavian artery'. Saved from 'the murderous Ghazis' by the devotion of his orderly, Murray, who threw Assistant-Surgeon Watson across a pack-horse and brought his master back to the British lines, the young doctor, after having nearly died of enteric, was invalided back to England. 'I was

Some stars of the contemporary music hall, all to be seen by Holmes at the Oxford

Vesta Tilley   Marie Lloyd   George Robey

Wilkie Bard   Dan Leno   Arthur Roberts

despatched, accordingly, to the troopship *Orontes,* and landed a
month later at Portsmouth jetty, with my health irretrievably ruined,
but with permission from a paternal government to spend the next
nine months in attempting to improve it.'

Watson, as the late William Baring-Gould has calculated, arrived
at Portsmouth on Friday, 26 November, 1880. Probably not more
than six weeks after this he met Holmes: it was as well that no
longer period elapsed since Watson, by his own confession, had
already encountered that menace which ever lies in wait for the
unattached, the idle, the aimless, the bored—over-spending.

> I had neither kith nor kin in England [this rather looks
> as though he *was* a Scotsman] and was therefore as free as
> air—or as free as an income of eleven shillings and sixpence
> a day will permit a man to be. Under such circumstances I
> naturally gravitated to London, that great cesspool into
> which all the loungers and idlers of the Empire are irresist-
> ibly drained. There I stayed for some time at a private hotel
> in the Strand, leading a comfortless, meaningless existence,
> and spending such money as I had, considerably more freely
> than I ought.

Watson was, he admits, over-spending to an extent where he must
decide to make a completely different way of life. Accepting the
choice of cutting his costs in London or going to 'rusticate somewhere in the country', he decided on the former; 'I began by making
up my mind to leave the hotel, and to take up my quarters in some
less pretentious and less expensive domicile'. Strand hotels were not,
at that time, notably expensive; even the Savoy, just opened, charged
only 8s for a single room and there were many good hotels charging
only 1s 6d or 2s a night.

On 11s 6d a day, a prudent Scotsman could have lived well, even
in the London of 1880. Eleven-and-six a day is four pounds and
sixpence a week. Many small hotels were advertising room, service
and two meals (breakfast and dinner) for thirty-five shillings a
week. Many were even cheaper. Watson would have had the choice
of innumerable restaurants offering three- and four-course luncheons
at anything between 8d and 1s 3d. His room, service, and all meals
need not have cost him more than two guineas a week. He would
have had nearly two pounds left to buy drink and tobacco. If one
wonders what drink cost in that far-off golden age, recall that, in
the adventure of 'The Noble Bachelor', Holmes is able to trace his

The Strand at Charing Cross Station in Holmes's day, still very little altered save that motor vehicles have replaced the horse-drawn traffic. The ' West Strand Telegraph Office ' on the ground floor of the building on the left is now a bank. On the extreme right is Charing Cross Hotel

quarry to one of the really top hotels in London—in newly-constructed Northumberland Avenue—because of a bill which shows that the hotel charges 8s for a room and 8d—as much as 8d! —for a cocktail. It could, Holmes pointed out, only have been a bill from one of London's most expensive hotels.

All the same Watson, with nothing to do, found that he could not exist on his eleven-and-sixpence a day and keep out of debt. When we first meet him, in the opening pages of 'A Study in Scarlet', he has not yet begun to economise—only to think of economising— and is in one of London's then more expensive bars: the American bar of the Criterion Hotel, still occupying most of the south side of Piccadilly Circus.

The 'Cri', then charging 5s for luncheon in the Byzantine Room, was definitely amongst London's dearer places, and though bottled Bass at 4d and Scotch and Irish whiskies at 4d, in a much larger measure than is sold today, do not strike us as profiteering prices, they were higher than other bars were charging. For instance, at the

Regent Street, 'Quadrant end' at the beginning of this century. The taxi-cab has already arrived, but the hansom is still with us. The names on the shops make clear that this was then one of the smartest streets in the world

Pavilion bar, just across the Circus (now a coffee-and-sandwich bar), they charged only 3d for bottled Bass, 3d for whiskies, and only 2½d for a bottle of Dublin-brewed Guinness's stout.

Outwardly, Piccadilly Circus has not changed greatly since that cold, bright day in January 1881 when Watson 'gravitated' into the 'Cri's' American bar, hungry for companionship, and there encountered 'young Stamford, who used to be my dresser at Bart's'.

The Pavilion music-hall is still standing—dingy now, with its classical façade permanently hidden by large signs announcing the films on show within, but it is still there. The Monico—it was never called, except by its proprietors, the Café Monico—has gone, though part of the building remains, housing shops which sell the sort of things one has come to expect to see on sale around Piccadilly Circus.

The Eros fountain, memorial to the seventh Earl of Shaftesbury, tireless champion of the sweated worker and a successful one, too!, is still there; but now hopeless drop-outs cover the always wet steps where, in the days up to the beginning of World War II, the Cockney flower girls sat by their vast baskets . . . 'Nice button-'ole, sir?' . . . 'Take some nice daffs 'ome for the Missus, Guv'?' . . . 'Fresh this morning, luvverly gladiolers!'

All but a few fragments of Nash's Regent Street and Regent Circus (as Piccadilly Circus was first called) went in the great rebuilding of Regent Street after the first World War. But now, fifty years after, the Reginald Bloomfield designs which replaced those of Nash are acquiring a charm of their own—compared with the plans which are being drawn up for the new 'two-tier' Piccadilly Circus. We can now see that Bloomfield's architecture wasn't half as bad as we thought; at least he sought to express, architecturally, the sentiment that he was designing for the principal street of the principal city of a great empire, not only drawing upon proven decorative motifs to clothe the steel carcases of his buildings, but acknowledging his debt to the past by effecting no dramatic break in style between his stone-faced six-storey fronts and the five-storey Nash stucco fronts they replaced.

It is still the fashion to deride the character of George IV, but it should be recalled that the construction of a wide street from the Regent's Park to Pall Mall was the result of an imaginative effort of private enterprise, carried out in partnership between

Picadilly Circus today. The still-surviving London Pavilion is almost hidden behind advertising signs; the remains of the extinct Café Monico (extreme left) completely so

George (not yet King) and John Nash, who was almost certainly George's illegitimate son.

The 'Government' had nothing to do with this venture, which provided a throughway slicing across a maze of old-fashioned, narrow streets, and raised the income of the areas thus 'improved' from hundreds to hundreds of thousands of pounds. George, having 'developed' Regent's Park, Portland Place, Langham Place, Regent Street (with its two 'Regent Circuses', north and south), Waterloo Place and much of Pall Mall—including Carlton House Terrace, built on the site of his own palace of Carlton House—turned his goldmine over to the Crown which now receives a rent for it from the government, itself no loser by the transaction.

Except for two of the original Nash stucco houses in Piccadilly Circus, hidden behind the neon signs which disfigure and disgrace

The gateway of St James's Palace, designed by Holbein in 1532, shown here as it was in 1890. Unaltered today, it is now dwarfed by the sky-scrapers which have arisen across St James's Park. The back of the Palace overlooks the Mall and Buckingham Palace

Yeomen of the Guard in their Tudor uniforms, parading in Friary Court,
St James's Palace. The picturesque dress of these royal guards, commonly
but erroneously called 'Beefeaters', dates from 1532, when Henry VIII
acquired St James's Palace

A squadron of Royal Life Guards in the Mall; Buckingham Palace, with the winged Victory of the Queen Victoria Memorial in the background

this 'Hub of the Empire', and stucco-fronted York Building (next to the Plaza cinema), which houses the West End office of the Cunard-White Star line, all of old Regent Street has gone. However, there is still much of the elegant Regency stucco left in and around Pall Mall, at one end of which is St James's Palace and the discreetly wealthy fashion which lives around Cleveland Row. At the other are classically rebuilt Waterloo Place and the still stuccoed end of the Haymarket, where the American Express Company, with unusual architectural good manners, rebuilt the bomb-demolished structure of Nash's day in a meticulously accurate reproduction deserving the highest praise. And even the New Zealand Government's deplorable concrete and glass skyscraper, which has replaced the old, elegant Carlton Hotel, still retains within its soul-less construction the groined ceiling and west side of a Regency shopping arcade, Royal Opera Arcade, built in 1820 to the designs of the Polish architect, Michael Novosielski, who also designed the Opera from which the still-existing arcade takes its name.

Pall Mall is still London's 'Street of Clubs' *par excellence,* and it was here that the Diogenes Club was to be found. It was, you may recall, the favourite (if not the only) club of Holmes's brother, Mycroft, a very senior civil servant in Her Majesty's Foreign Service, and a man whose work was so important to the well-being of Crown and Realm that, in talking of Mycroft's status, Holmes permitted himself to be enthusiastically complimentary far beyond his usual reticence. There has been considerable rebuilding in Pall Mall since the end of the last century, and the Diogenes Club has been swept away, but the remaining clubs, especially the stucco-fronted ones on the south side nearer to St James's Palace, will give you a good idea of what the Diogenes Club looked like in the 1880s. On your way to St James's Palace, pause for a moment outside the reconstructed seventeenth-century Schomberg House, where Thomas Gainsborough once lived. In the reign of William III, this former Cromwellian military headquarters was the residence of Frederick, first, and last, Duke of Schomberg, one of the Dutch king's generals and the only Jew ever to have become a field-marshal of the British Army. Schomberg was killed in 1690 at the Battle of the Boyne.

What ought to interest the passer-by more is the fact that it was in this house, at the end of the following century, that the notorious

Also in the Mall: a company of Foot Guards, with a squadron of Life Guards in the rear. In the distance: the Admiralty Arch which, together with the fountain before Buckingham Palace, forms part of the national memorial to Queen Victoria (1819-1901)

'Doctor' Graham, one of the first practising sexologists of history, ran his catch-penny fertility clinic, in which he charged childless married couples £100 a night to sleep in his 'magnetic Celestial Bed'. Naked come-on girls clearly indicated the true nature of this bizarre establishment; one of them, Emma Lyon, went on to far greater things—as Emma Hamilton, wife of His Majesty's Minister to the Court of Naples and mistress of (amongst many others) Lord Nelson. Emma has now joined that mythological band of strumpets who are more admired than the good women whose hearts they broke.

Mycroft Holmes worked in the Foreign Office, built at a cost of £500,000 (say £10,000,000, at least, in today's dodgy currency) between 1868 and 1873. Designed by Sir Gilbert Scott 'in the Italian manner', the still surviving and now somewhat dingy Foreign Office is one of London's nobler buildings, which is why it is being per-

The Foreign Office, seen from across the lake in St. James's Park, at the time when Holmes was a frequent visitor there

mitted to fall into, if not decay, then shabbiness, so that 'redevelop-
ment' may profitably take place. It was a new building when
Mycroft, leaving the F.O. by the Downing Street entrance, walked
across St James's Park to Pall Mall, to read *The Times* and take
his *apéritif* sherry-and-bitters in the Diogenes Club, whilst his
younger brother, Sherlock, walked down newly cut but not yet
constructed Charing Cross Road, on his way to lay a problem
before his older and (it is Sherlock's own admission) far more
erudite and worldly brother.

It has been suggested that the name 'Diogenes' conceals the
identity of the famed Athenaeum Club, founded in 1824 and built
on its present site in 1829 to the designs of Decimus Burton,
architect of the fine stone screen at the southern, Constitutional Hill,
entrance to Hyde Park. 'Diogenes' may well stand for 'Athenaeum',
since it was at Athens that the Cynic philosopher, Diogenes, became
the disciple of Antisthenes.

If, then, 'Diogenes' should really be 'Athenaeum', we know that
Mycroft left the Foreign Office by the Downing Street entrance,
crossed the gravelled Horse Guards parade ground, crossed the
Mall to Duke of York Steps and so entered, on the left-hand side,
the still standing and still exclusive Athenaeum Club, over whose
severely Regency-classical portico broods a bust of Pallas, as it did
over the chamber-door of Poe's anonymous raven-attractor.

Standing on the Duke of York's Steps, with Nash's Carlton
House Terrace to right and left, and looking across St James's Park
at Kent's Horse Guards (1758), the back of the old Admiralty
(1725—Sir Aston Webb's addition was not completed until 1896),
the Scottish Office (Kent, 1758, but the very elegant Whitehall
front dates from 1816), the Treasury (1846-7), Downing Street
(1681, but reconstructed since) and the Foreign Office (1868-73), it
is hard to believe that nearly a century has passed since young Mr
Holmes came down—without a degree—from his university to 'win
or lose it all' in the fiercely competitive, fiercely jealous, unrelent-
ingly snobbish London of 1878.

For, as we stand on the Steps, beneath the 124 ft granite column,
erected by public subscription of £25,000 to the memory of
Frederick, Duke of York, second son of George III, we see, almost
unaltered, what Mycroft and Sherlock saw in 1878: across the
smooth lawns and past the weeping willows and over the raked

View of the Duke of York's Steps, looking south from Waterloo Place. Mycroft Holmes, who had chambers and a club in Pall Mall, must often have used these steps going to and from his important job at the Foreign Office

golden gravel—the nerve-centre of an empire that Mycroft was already serving, and which, in the not-so-distant future, Sherlock would come to serve with even more skill, though hardly with greater devotion.

That empire that Sherlock and Mycroft—and Watson, too—served has now gone; but the Crown which has symbolised and centralised the realm since England was united under the kings of Wessex—that remains.

To their right, as they stood on the Steps, Mycroft and Sherlock could see, at the end of the tree-lined Mall, the London palace of the sovereign—what Queen Victoria, in her whimsical way, used to refer to, disparagingly, as 'our little cottage in Pimlico'.

In 1878 Buckingham Palace was a vast Regency pile, more beautiful within than without, and bearing everywhere the mark of the builder-king (or, rather, builder-prince), George IV. Nash's Palladian front, constructed between 1826 and 1836, did not appeal to the immediately succeeding monarchs, and in 1846 a decidedly ugly east front was added to the palace by the architect, James Blore, at a cost of £150,000. A south wing, with ballroom, was added in 1856; the ballroom, still one of the most imposing in the world, measures 111 ft by 60 ft.

Surplus funds having accumulated from the public subscription to the Queen Victoria memorial which now stands before the palace (the memorial also included ornamental stonework and metal railings hemming the circle around the statue), it was decided to provide the palace with a new front, more in keeping with the status of a sovereign who was then emperor as well as king. Long before the latest improvements, the Marble Arch, which had formerly stood, in Nash's design, as an entrance gate to the palace, was removed to Cumberland Gate, Hyde Park, where it still is.

Sir Aston Webb's refronting was a miracle of high-speed work. By careful 'pre-fabrication' of the numbered elements, the imposing stone front was placed in position whilst King George V and Queen Mary were 'out of town'. Begun in August 1912, the work was completed in time for Their Majesties' return to the palace in the November of that year.

The unaffected monarch, who never hesitated to display either his pleasure or his irritation, was so delighted with the speed and quality of the alterations to his London home that he commanded

A FACE LIFT FOR THE PALACE

With surplus funds remaining after the Victoria Memorial had been erected in front
Buckingham Palace, a new facade was provided for the palace itself. The ugly Victoria
front was covered with a stone facing in a classical design by Sir Aston Webb, tl
whole work being completed in the record time of exactly three months. Here a
three views of the palace front since the days when Holmes was first commanded to
private audience of Her Majesty Queen Victoria

The original east front of Buckingham Palace,
built by James Blore, in 1846, at a cost of
£150,000

(*Right*) The re-
fronted palace,
as it appeared
immediately after
the completion of
the new facade,
modelled on that
of the Grand Du-
cal Palace, Bruns-

wick, in Noven
ber 1912. (*Below*
Buckingham P
lace today, r
stored after
wartime boml
ing, seen acro
St James's Par

all who had been concerned, from Sir Aston to the humblest cement-mixer, to sit down to dinner with their king in the palace they had all helped to beautify.

There has been much adverse criticism of the new front: I once heard the late Michael Arlen get a laugh by appearing to defend the Victoria Memorial—'After all', he said, 'it *does* help to hide the palace's new front'. He liked the remark so much that he later put it into one of his books.

The criticism is unjustified. I am not a committed admirer of Sir Aston Webb's work and think his Admiralty Arch indifferent stuff indeed, but I know of no architecture that more truthfully records the sentiments of British society in the years immediately preceding the first World War than the stone front he gave to Buckingham Palace. It is even more truthful, more honest, in that it betrays a candid nostalgia, since it so obviously seeks to recall the ducal palace of Brunswick, to which royal house the greatest developer of Buckingham Palace, George IV, belonged.

The stucco buildings to the left, as one looks at the palace, are the barracks of the Guards—Wellington Barracks. Amongst them is an obviously modern building: this is the Guards' chapel, successor to that destroyed one Sunday morning in June 1944 by a German flying-bomb. Nearly two hundred people were in the chapel that sunny morning, with the Colonel, Lord Edward Hay, reading the Lesson as the bomb burst through the roof, exploding amongst the congregation and bringing most of the building down upon them in ruins.

Within ten years of his coming to London, Sherlock Holmes, self-styled 'private consulting detective', would overcome many a deep prejudice against his manner and 'profession', and become intimately acquainted with all those important buildings to be seen from the steps of the Duke of York's Column: the Imperial German Embassy in nearby Carlton House Terrace, the Admiralty, the Foreign Office, the Treasury, and even Buckingham Palace itself. Royalty—British and otherwise—would call on him again and again, and he would never fail to produce the required solution to a problem involving the highest affairs of state.

Even before Sherlock met Watson, in the early January of 1881, Holmes had been called in by the British Admiralty in the affair of the Bruce-Partington plans; but within that ten years from starting,

Holmes's royal clients were to include the King of Scandinavia (probably March 1881), (The Delicate Affair of) the Reigning Family of Holland (between November 1886 and January 1887); the hereditary King of Bohemia (20-22 May 1887); and almost certainly Albert Edward, Prince of Wales, later King Edward VII ('The Atrocious Conduct of Colonel Upwood in Connection with the Famous Card Scandal at the Nonpareil Club', between Saturday, 20 October and late November 1888). The Prince's addiction to (then illegal) card games involving very high stakes resulted in several scandals, not all of which had the advantage of being cleared up by Holmes—the Tranby Croft baccarat scandal, which brought the prince into the witness-box against the colonel of the Grenadier Guards, Colonel Sir William Gordon-Cumming, is a case in point. This was unfortunate, but I see from the record that, at the time when Holmes's tact could have kept the facts of the Tranby Croft affair from the public sheets, he was taken up with that mysterious 'Matter of Supreme Importance to the French Government' (late December 1890 to March 1891).

Holmes's connection with the affair of Colonel Upwood brought him, of course, into contact with the Brigade of Guards at their most spankingly aristocratic: some of the less imaginative subalterns must have been hard put to it to bear some of Sherlock's more unconventional mannerisms with well-bred tolerance. Republican as well as royal governments sought his aid—the royal family of Scandinavia summoned him again to their aid in late December 1890; and one feels that, since it happened in Jubilee Year, 1887, when the cloudless weather pleaded for *no more scandals, please!*, Holmes's saving of Colonel Prendergast's good name in the Tankerville Club Scandal must have involved him, not only with the Brigade of Guards but with our own royalty as well.

And whatever Holmes's religious affiliations, the Pope himself did not hesitate to call on him for help: there were the affairs of the Vatican Cameos (between April and May 1888) and far more important, Holmes's investigation of the sudden death of Cardinal Tosca. Few professional careers can have proved so successful so quickly, and it is not to underrate Sherlock's ability to suggest that he must have owed many of his earlier influential clients to Mycroft's introductions.

CHAPTER 2

Fellow-lodgers in Baker Street

Once, with a reverent air befitting the occasion, senior members of the Sherlock Holmes Society of London, including Lord Donegall and the late Sir Sydney Roberts, stood on the rather windy corner of Piccadilly Circus and Lower Regent Street gazing at a handsome bronze plaque which had just been unveiled. Fastened to the wall of 'the new part of the Criterion Hotel, it recorded the meeting of Watson with 'young Stamford' in the American bar of 'the Cri'. Some years ago, the plaque disappeared: only four holes now remain in the stone to mark where it once 'marked the spot'. However, the bronze plate inside St Bartholomew's Hospital has not yet been stolen, and there is no reason to suppose that it will be.

Of course it was of vital importance that, having decided to alter his way of living, Watson should have strolled into the 'Cri' bar in January 1881 and there met the one man who could have taken him to meet Sherlock Holmes:

> . . . a fellow who is working at the chemical laboratory up at the hospital. He was bemoaning himself this morning because he could not get someone to go halves with him in some nice rooms which he had found, and which were too much for his purse. 'By Jove!' I cried; 'if he really wants someone to share the rooms and the expense, I am the very man for him. I should prefer having a partner to being alone'.

'Young Stamford', we recall, instantly gave warning—'You don't know Sherlock Holmes yet; perhaps you would not care for him as a constant companion . . .'

AT THIS PLACE NEW YEARS DAY, 1881
WERE SPOKEN THESE DEATHLESS WORDS

"YOU HAVE BEEN
IN AFGHANISTAN, I PERCEIVE."
BY
Mr. SHERLOCK HOLMES
IN GREETING TO
JOHN H. WATSON, M.D.
AT THEIR FIRST MEETING

THE BAKER STREET IRREGULARS — 1953
BY THE AMATEUR MENDICANTS AT THE CAUCUS CLUB.

Bronze plaque in the Pathological Laboratory of St Bartholomew's Hospital, commemorating the meeting of Holmes and Watson in ' Bart's ' in early January 1881

The warning fell on deaf ears: Watson, having made up his mind to economise, was prepared to risk the discomforts of incompatibility; the fact is, as is clear from Watson's only half-concealed blabbing, he was in a state not far off panic. He *had* to economise, and here, in 'young Stamford's' suggestion of a fellow-lodger, was the chance the desperate man craved. He *had* to share with Sherlock. So Watson listens to Stamford's halting attempt to explain Holmes's 'queerness'—and 'I should like to meet him', says Watson. 'If I am to lodge with anyone, I should prefer a man of studious and quiet habits . . . How could I meet this friend of yours?'

So they lunch at the Holborn restaurant—then 2s 6d—and, since Watson uses the expression 'made our way to the hospital', they probably walk the half-mile from the corner of Little Queen Street to St Sepulchre (where Capt John Smith of Virginia lies buried twenty-five miles from where his beloved Pocahontas sleeps her eternal sleep) along a High Holborn, Holborn and Newgate Street narrower and older than our own. High Holborn then had two first-class hotels in it—the Inns of Court and the First Avenue—

the first offering 'ascending rooms for the convenience of guests', and the latter 'the electric light in all parts of the hotel'.

Part of the Inns of Court frontage in Lincoln's Inn Fields survived until 1936; in its day, this was amongst the largest and most luxurious hotels in London. Built in 1866, it was three years younger than the Langham.

Holborn Bars was still late medieval and Restoration in aspect: the black-and-white timber-framed houses, a handful of which (with reinforced concrete innards) still survive around the entrance to Staple Inn, extended in 1881, from Finch's old wine lodge, destroyed

The Chemical Laboratory, St Bartholomew's Hospital. It was here that Holmes was experimenting with his 'infallible blood test' when Stamford introduced him to Dr Watson

Late sixteenth-century ' black and white ' gabled houses in Holborn facing the southern end of Gray's Inn Road. Holmes must have passed these old houses, still standing today, many times on his way from Montague Street to ' Bart's '

only two or three years ago, to Thavies Inn. The London of 1881 was a London rich in the means to eat and drink—a fact easy to understand when it is noted that there are now over 50,000 *fewer* licensed premises than there were in 1900. Holborn, in particular, was full of chop-houses (Keen's was a favourite), oyster-bars (favourite was Driver's, at the top of Chancery Lane), wine lodges (besides the two Finch's—different firms—there was the not yet rebuilt Henekey's at the Holborn entrance to Gray's Inn). Gamages had not yet arrived, but there was the big department store of Thomas Wallis and Co, destroyed by bombing in 1940, in Holborn Circus. Altogether, in High Holborn and Holborn, there were fifty licensed premises against the dozen of today.

The strongly antique flavour grew as one neared Smithfield, the Charterhouse and Cloth Fair, and even more so in narrow streets like Little Britain, which seemed to huddle around the great bulk of St Bartholomew's Hospital.

Craven House, Baker Street, a contender for the claim to be the original of '221B' where, in 1881, Holmes and Watson set up housekeeping together

Lying between Giltspur Street and Little Britain, St Bartholomew's Hospital, said to have been founded in 1123 by Rahere, jester to King Henry I, is, if not of direct Roman foundation, at least raised on the well-preserved and extensive remains of a Roman building. The crypt of its wonderful Norman church is Roman without a doubt. Though having been considerably enlarged even since 1881, the hospital still retains, despite 're-development' and despite bombing, the appearance it must have had when Watson, who already knew it well, went there in 1881 to meet Holmes. He met him in the chemical laboratory, which has altered a good deal, though not so much as to be unrecognisable to Watson and Holmes were they to return.

It was one of the great meetings of the world: comparable, not only in importance but also in a sort of intrinsically dramatic quality, with that handful of other meetings we have agreed to see

109 Baker Street; the last remaining house in this street to have preserved
its original facade. Occupied for many years by the well-known firm of
Richards & Co., solicitors, it has been carefully restored by Haslemere
Estates, specialists in the praiseworthy task of adapting old property to
modern use

as of a quite extraordinary quality: Dante's first encounter with Beatrice, Boswell's introduction to Dr Johnson in the back parlour of Tom Davies's bookshop, Livingstone's meeting with Stanley.

What the meeting of Holmes and Watson had in common with all other singularly memorable and undeniably important first meetings was the dramatic brevity of the script: ' "Dr Watson, Mr Sherlock Holmes", said Stamford, introducing us. "How are you?" he said cordially, gripping my hand with a strength for which I should hardly have given him credit. "You have been in Afghanistan, I perceive." '

With those few words began the second greatest literary partnership in the world. On the following day, Watson accompanied Holmes to see the lodgings of which Stamford had spoken. 'I have my eye on a suite in Baker Street which would suit us down to the ground. You don't mind the smell of strong tobacco, I hope?'

And so it was settled. The accommodation at 221B Baker Street—

. . . consisted of a couple of comfortable bedrooms and a single large airy sitting-room, cheerfully furnished, and illuminated by two broad windows. So desirable in every way were the apartments, and so moderate did the terms seem when divided between us, that the bargain was concluded on the spot, and we at once entered into possession.

That very evening I moved my things round from the hotel, and on the following morning Sherlock Holmes followed me with several boxes and portmanteaus. For a day or two we were busily employed in unpacking and laying out our property to the best advantage. That done, we gradually began to settle down and to accommodate ourselves to our new surroundings.

Thus quietly did the most famous address in the world enter into men's consciousness. I have calculated elsewhere that Mrs Hudson, the landlady who provided cooking and cleaning within the rent, probably charged the two men £4, or perhaps four guineas, between them; but further researches have let me consider a lower sum than this, and it is not unlikely that, for a 'permanency', Mrs Hudson need have charged not more than £3 'all in'.

As regards the situation, it was even more convenient for Holmes than 24 Montague Street had been. Traffic facilities were excellent: from the Baker Street station of the Metropolitan Railway, Holmes could catch an underground (steam-driven) train to Aldersgate

Baker Street Station in the 1890s. From here, Holmes and Watson caught the train to many a London adventure

Station, itself but a few minutes' walk from Bart's. Buses—horse-drawn, of course—ran briskly and frequently along Baker Street and the Marylebone Road, as they do today, save that there was then no 'one-way' system, and buses could be caught—one hailed them as one does a taxi today—on any street, going in either direction. One of Holmes's favourite buses must have been the green 'Atlas', which ran down Baker Street, along Orchard Street, turned left, past the stone-fronted, six-storey Somerset Hotel, at what is now Selfridge's big department store (building commenced 1907, completed 1928) and so along Oxford Street, through the shabby western end, passing the narrow entrance to Marylebone Lane, through the smart 'Ladies' Mile' to Oxford Circus and so down Regent Street to Piccadilly Circus.

The Great Central Line—and so Great Central Station—had not yet been built when Watson and Holmes took up their residence in Baker Street in January 1881; but buses ran frequently along the Marylebone Road to Paddington Station, a terminus with which many of Holmes's cases were to make the men familiar. To cite two of the best known cases: that of *The Hound of the Baskervilles*

(Tuesday, 25 September to Saturday, 20 October 1888) and that of 'Silver Blaze' (Thursday, 25 September to Tuesday, 30 September 1890).

Of course, as Watson was unemployed, one London address was as convenient as another to him. There were many ways of filling in his time, besides acting as amanuensis and historian to Holmes. At Nos 56-58 Baker Street, for example, there were the Portman Rooms and Baker Street Bazaar, a double-fronted house which contained Madame Tussaud's Waxworks Exhibition. Not long after the two men had taken up their residence at No 221B, the exhibition moved to its own hall in the Marylebone Road, where, though damaged by fire in 1925, it still is. A planetarium has been added to the attractions that the waxworks provide. The old hall, I remember, used to display, among its other 'curiosities', the closed carriage in which the despairing Napoleon drove from the field of Waterloo. Children, in my young days, were permitted to enter—for the appropriate fee, of course—this ill-smelling but historic

The old ' Buffalo's Head ' public-house, seen just before demolition in 1911

antiquity, and I myself sat on the faded cloth seat where the Little Corporal had sat a century before. It was sad that, of all the relics rescued during that fire of 1925, the carriage of Napoleon should have been missing from the tally.

And if Watson was not above taking his drop ('Young Stamford looked rather strangely at me over his wine-glass . . .'), there were many bars and public-houses in the neighbourhood to which he could take his thirst. Many have gone, amongst them the cozy 'Buffalo's Head', next door to Baker Street station in the Marylebone Road, and now absorbed into the block of flats, Chiltern Court, which rises above the reconstructed station. But the 'Beehive' with its original late Georgian upper storeys, the 'Barley Mow', the 'Apollo' and several other survivals from the days of Holmes and Watson, are still doing business on the old pitch.

Watson need not have felt lonely when waiting for Holmes to return from one of his cases, though I feel that, after living in Baker Street for two months, the pubs and Madame Tussaud's had so lost their attraction for Watson that it was at his suggestion that Holmes invited him to accompany him, on 4 March 1881, to the Brixton Road, in the opening movement of 'A Study in Scarlet' ('A most extraordinary case—a most incomprehensible affair'). For it is clear that, in several cases Holmes had handled after Watson had joined him as co-lodger at 221B, he had *not* invited Watson to join him. Some at least of the following must have occurred *after* Watson had come to live with Holmes: 'The Tarleton Murders', 'The Case of Vamberry, the Wine Merchant', 'The Adventure of the Old Russian Woman', 'The Singular Affair of the Aluminium Crutch', 'Rigoletti of the Club Foot and his Abominable Wife', 'The Trifling Affair of Mortimer Maberley', 'The Taking of Brooks and Woodhouse', 'The *Matilda Briggs* and the Giant Rat of Sumatra', 'The Case of Mrs Farintosh and an Opal Tiara', and a case which may be dated to late February 1881 and so definitely post-Watsonian, the forgery case to which allusion is made in 'A Study in Scarlet'. Boredom with his own company had turned Watson, in no very long time, to seek interest in the odd activities of his fellow-lodger.

When Holmes and Watson decided to club together in what the former called a 'suite of rooms' in Baker Street, that street was not as long as it is today. It ran from Portman Square to that cross street which is Crawford Street on the west and Paddington Street on the east. From Crawford Street to the Marylebone Road, Baker Street (if I may so express it) became York Place, a name which survives in that of a block of flats, York Place Mansions. Then, crossing the Marylebone Road, York Place changed its name and became Upper Baker Street. No '221B' is, of course, an imaginary number—the Baker Street numbers ran from No 1 to No 84, so that there could never have been a '221B'. Many researchers of a speculative fancy—the present writer included—have sought to determine which of the Baker Street houses harboured the Holmes-Watson household, but it is only fair to say that, for all the many plausible claimants to the honour of having been the original of '221B', an unassailable case has never yet been made out. The definitive solution is still to come.

In those days, commerce had already come to Baker Street, as a glance at *The Post Office London Directory* of the relevant years will show; but York Place, even in 1881, was still 'strictly residential'—that last section of what we now call 'Baker Street' to succumb to the relentless pressure of money-chasing. Local councils, who get higher rates from business premises than from private dwellings, naturally welcome and, if they can, accelerate the change. But when Holmes and Watson first took rooms in Baker Street, York Place was still the 'better section'. Wherever '221B' may have been in Baker Street, the 'B' shows that it was over a shop or office. The one absolutely essential qualification that any claimant address must have is that the rooms shall back on to a mews.

One difficulty in identifying '221B' is Watson's reference to a 'bow window' in their sitting-room. No *upstairs* window in Baker Street can ever have been accurately described as 'bow', though several ground-floor shops have had them, some dating from the eighteenth century, some modern but self-consciously 'antique'. But not on the first (what Americans call the 'second') floor. Here the tall windows have either flat tops or round-headed arches—is this possibly what Watson means when he talks about 'bow' windows?

I had an aunt who had a cat. The cat was spiteful, and its ill temper was explained to me as the result of the cat's 'being set in its ways'. I feel that Holmes's frequent sarcasms and even outright

insolence would have been explained by my aunt as the result of
his being 'set in his ways'.

Few who have read of Sherlock Holmes's adventures carry away
with them the impression of his relative youth. Born in 1854, in
Yorkshire, he was only twenty-seven when he met and teamed up
with Watson, even though seven years had passed since the solution
of his first case, that of 'The *Gloria Scott*'.

The fact is that Holmes seems to be one of those born, as they
say, 'beyond his years'. Certainly his gravity often appears more
suited to a man thrice his age. And, indeed, he himself, apparently
aware of this, contributes to the impression of age-beyond-his-
years. For instance, though only thirty-three when he relieves the
hereditary King of Bohemia from the anxiety caused by his writing
of indiscreet letters and of posing for indiscreet photographs ('I was
only Crown Prince then. I was young . . .'), Holmes seems to affect
an experienced attitude certainly not justified by his age.

'. . . . Your Highness*, as I understand, became entangled with
this young person, wrote her some compromising letters, and is now
desirous of getting these letters back?'

The 'young person' to whom Holmes refers was the lady whom
the king describes as 'the well-known adventuress, Irene Adler'.
But Irene, whom the smitten Holmes was later to call 'the daintiest
thing under a bonnet on this planet', was born in 1858, and was
thus twenty-nine when her menaces drove the King of Bohemia to
seek Holmes's aid. Yet Holmes, though but thirty-three, refers to
her as 'this young person'.

It is this 'born old' attitude towards men and things which must
account for Holmes's general—though not, as I shall point out,
total—prejudice against 'new fangled' attitudes and appliances. He
is dead set against slack manners: he is, one observes, quick to
rebuke what he thinks is the over-familiarity of Baron Adalbert
Gruner ('The Adventure of the Illustrious Client') and the very
much lesser lights from Scotland Yard are constantly being put in
their place for one slip or another. Holmes cannot even refrain
from passing a critical eye over the Foreign Secretary, Lord Holdhurst ('The Case of the Naval Treaty'), though, as a well-bred man,
Holmes reserves his criticism until after the two friends have left

---

*Holmes commits no solecism here: the king has called on Holmes incognito as
'Count von Kramm'.

the F.O. 'Did you observe, Watson, *that his boots had been mended?*'

It is this prejudice against novelty, of manner or of invention, which conditions, I feel, his attitude towards the telephone. Though the electro-magnetic telephone had been invented by Johan Philipp Reis in 1860 and successfully demonstrated by him in 1861, his was not a commercially practical instrument, which came, about 1877, through the combined inventiveness of Gray, Graham Bell and Edison. In 1879 Edison opened London's first telephone exchange in Lombard Street, near where the General Post Office had been since Cromwell's day, until moved to its present site at St Martin's-le-Grand in 1874. The speed with which the enterprising Edison put this new invention on the market says much for his commercial acumen; it was a speed, though, matched by that with which the public accepted the telephone as a factor of everyday living.

I take this from the Goncourts' *Journal,* under date Thursday, 5 January 1882, exactly one year after Watson and Holmes had set up their joint home in Baker Street:

> Bing's head clerk gave his employer notice to-day . . .
> by telephone. Yes, by *telephone!* It's the very latest thing,
> this new method of taking leave. It certainly cuts out all
> possibility of argument!

But however much the Goncourts were impressed by the telephone and however rapidly the Parisians had assimilated the new instrument of communication to their commercial and private lives, Holmes found the telephone far too novel for *his* acceptance.

When did they finally submit, and have the telephone installed in Baker Street? Or, rather, when did Holmes consent to its installation, since, to Watson, the instrument must have seemed a Godsend from the moment of its birth. Nine years after Edison's first telephone exchange had been opened in Lombard Street ('the lady operators are under the constant supervision of a lady superintendent'), we find Holmes crossing the road to use the telephone in the post-office. This is in 1888, when he has already been called in for assistance by the British and Russian governments and no fewer than four royal families!

The first actual mention of a telephone being in No 221B is in Watson's account of 'The Adventure of the Retired Colourman', which may be dated at July 1898, nearly twenty years after Edison had brought the telephone to London and sixteen years after Bing, the Parisian curio-dealer's head clerk, had sacked himself on the telephone. Of course, there may have been a telephone at 221B before 1898; Watson may merely not have mentioned the fact. But I think not: there *was* one invention to which I shall presently return—the *gazogène*—which was permitted by the novelty-hating Holmes, and Watson mentions *that*.

No, I think that the absence of Watson's mention of a telephone at 221B in the earlier cases is simply explained by the fact that Holmes disliked the 'new fangled' telephone, wouldn't have it at any price, and found that, apart from personal calls (usually by hansom or four-wheeler), the telegram served all his communication needs, especially when he had Watson or 'our boy in buttons' to run across the road with it.

There were many reasons of a practical nature why Holmes should have relied on the telegram; it was not all prejudice on his part which disinclined him to substitute the telephone for the telegram. In the first place, the telegram was quick. The Post Office, in those days, set out to offer a service, and saw to it that its servants actually served the public, not merely treated themselves as pensionaries of the Post Office or 'supporters' of the Union of Post Office Workers.

It was also inexpensive—a merely token sixpence for twelve words: a halfpenny a word—and somehow one feels that Watson's Scots habits must have come in handy in keeping the exuberance and irrelevance out of Holmes's telegraphic style. The undeniable advantage of the telegram, until the end of the Post Office's golden age in 1939, was that the Post Office endeavoured to deliver the telegram as quickly as possible. And, of course, that meant delivering it personally at any time of the day or night; not merely shoving it through a letter-box and then only during 'working hours'. Whereas the telephone depended on the operator at the exchange, and only the very clearest lines were then free of the buzz and clatter and fog which made telephoning a duty to be undertaken only in necessity. Victorian practicality never showed itself to greater advantage than in its organising of the telegraph service.

In the new (1874) General Post Office at St Martin's-le-Grand, erected at a cost of nearly £500,000, the vast building complex, hit and badly damaged during the second World War, was divided

House of Commons interior, about 1887. Designed by Sir Charles Barry, the rich Victorian Gothic decoration and furnishing were completely destroyed by fire in an air-raid of 10 May 1941. The rebuilt debating chamber was officially opened by the late King George VI on 26 October 1950

into two principal sections: General Post Office East and General Post Office West. Post Office West was necessitated by the government's having taken over all telegraphs, except the private wires of the railway companies, in 1870.

Occupying all the upper floors of General Post Office West, the telegraph department, within ten years of the take-over, was employing 3,000 telegraph operators and servicing 1,500 instruments of various types. 'The principal instruments in use at the office are the single-needle, the Morse inker, the Hughes and the Wheatstone's automatic . . . The Hughes instrument is most readily appreciated by strangers, as it records the message in actual Roman type'.

This incredibly efficient system was housed in the Metropolitan Gallery of General Post Office West, and even as early as 1870 a large proportion of the operators were women.

> In the telegraph department of the new wing young ladies are seated at long rows of tables crossing the room from end to end, and, with few exceptions, each one has before her a single needle or printing instrument, the 'circuit', or place with which it is in communication, being denoted on a square tablet, something like a headstone in a cemetery, erected immediately in front of her. It may further be remarked of these young ladies, that they talk much less than might be expected, work very quickly, and have generally very nice hands.

But it was in the collection and distribution of the messages at maximum speed that Victorian inventiveness and avocational honesty showed themselves at their best.

> In addition to the fifteen hundred instruments, the three thousand operators, and the special arrangements for making through connections with different parts of the kingdom, a most interesting room is the chamber given up to the pneumatic tubes.

> All London messages pass through the Central, and for this purpose it has been found that these tubes are quicker even than electricity. Powerful engines exhaust the air in the tubes, and then when the signal is given, say at Charing Cross, a handle is turned, and in three minutes a thud is heard, and out of the pipe is taken a cylinder made of felt, which may contain thirty or forty messages on the forms

House of Lords interior, about 1887. This noble chamber, also the work of Barry, escaped the bombing which destroyed much of the House of Commons. Holmes had intimate professional contacts with members of both Houses of Parliament

The restored Houses of Parliament as they are today. In the centre is
Westminster Hall, rebuilt by Richard II in 1397; on the right is the House
of Commons, on the left the House of Lords. The largest Gothic edifice
in the world, the Palace of Westminster has five hundred apartments,
eleven open courts, eighteen official residences and the two Houses of
Parliament. It took nineteen years to build and cost £3,000,000. Much
more has since been spent on repair

upon which they were handed in at Charing Cross. They
are at once distributed and despatched very much sooner
than they could possibly have been from the local centre.
This method is, however, available only for short distances,
the longest tube being that which connects the Post Office
with the House of Commons.

The same system is in use today, with the pneumatic tubes
extending to up to six miles from the General Post Office.

Some idea of the standards of speed which the Post Office of
close on a century ago set up for itself and conscientiously maintained—standards certainly not confined to the British Post Office
—may be gained from this quotation from Walter Thornbury's *Old
and New London* (*c.* 1880) : —

Familiar ground to Holmes: Holborn Circus and Holborn Viaduct, as they were when Holmes was going daily to 'Bart's'. The spectacle-sign on the extreme left marks the shop of Negretti & Zambra, famous makers of optical instruments; it was almost certainly from this shop that Holmes bought his microscope, mentioned in 'The Case of Shoscombe Old Place' and his magnifying glasses ('lens') mentioned not fewer than twenty-two times in the record

Pausing for an instant by the side of the young lady . . . we find her at fifty-four and a half minutes past three pm writing off the last words of a message which had been handed in at the office on Holborn Viaduct at fifty-three minutes past three pm, *and which will thus have been completed and ready for sending out for delivery within two minutes.**

Lavish user of telegrams though he was, there was a section of the Telegraph Department which must have handled more of Holmes's messages than any other:

Here, in this south-western division, are what are known as the 'official circuits', worked by the A.B.C. instrument, with the grinding handle and the depressible alphabetical keys familiar to most of us, which communicate with the War Office, the Foreign Office, the Treasury, the Admiralty,

---

*My italics—M.H.

The 'new' War Office in Whitehall, erected between 1899 and 1906 at a cost of £1,000,000. Designed by William Young, this handsome stone-faced building replaced the dingy old War Department office in Pall Mall. With both the old and new War Offices, Holmes's work at top government level must have made him familiar

the Houses of Parliament and the whipper-in.

Here, too, is the last specimen left throughout the building of what at one time used to be the favourite telegraphic instrument, the 'double needle', which is used for communication with Buckingham Palace. At Windsor, Osborne and Balmoral there are telegraphic instruments, under the charge of a clerk, who travels with the Court, to which he has been attached for some years; while Sandringham,* Badminton, the seat of the Chancellor of the Exchequer at Caterham, and the country houses of various other noblemen and officials, are similarly furnished.

With his passion for keeping accurate time, it is a wonder that Holmes could resist having his apartments connected up with the—

. . . chronopher, or instrument from which all England is supplied with the correct time . . . Messrs Dent, Benson, and all the principal watchmakers in London receive the time every hour from this chronopher. Time-guns at New-

*Country seat of the Prince of Wales.

castle and at Shields are also fired at 1 pm by batteries connected with the chronopher at the (Post) office, the clock attached to which is regulated for accuracy to the twentieth part of a second.

Holmes succeeded in his self-chosen profession because he was fortunate enough to have had the opportunity to begin in a period which appreciated the genuine, rather than the bogus. Beginning to-day, he would, however talented, have had to put himself in debt for slick offices and an array of electronic gadgets—better to-day to fail because the computer let you down than succeed with nothing more than the intelligence that God gave you.

The *gazogène*—spelt 'gasogene' in the Canon—is mentioned only in two cases: that of 'A Scandal in Bohemia' and 'The Adventure of the Mazarin Stone'. It is curious, then, to note that this ingenious producer of carbonated water is certainly amongst the better known of the furnishings of 221B. Even the fact that there are fourteen

The old War Office, then called the Ordnance Office, in Pall Mall. It moved—as the War Department—to Whitehall in 1899

or fifteen references to alcoholic drinks in the Canon—apart from the reference to 'the spirit-case' in 'A Scandal in Bohemia'—hardly explains how it is that two references to the *gazogène* should have made it so well known. Still, well known it is, and though we may date 'A Scandal in Bohemia' as in Golden Jubilee Year, 1887, I feel that the *gazogène,* first mentioned in this case, must have been acquired by Holmes and/or Watson much earlier in their joint tenancy of 221B.

The *gazogène* is certainly a gadget; it is no less certainly a novelty. Why, then, did Holmes accept it, with all its novelty, all its gadgetry, when he resolutely turned his face from the telephone? The answer which suggests itself is that, for all its 'new fangled-ness', the *gazogène* not only worked but could be shown to be able to work.

Though more than a decade was to pass before Holmes accepted, almost certainly from the hands of Casimir-Perrier, President of the

Whitehall's most famous building: the last remaining (visible) portion of the old Palace of White Hall: the Banqueting Hall, built by Inigo Jones in 1622. It was from a window of this elegant building that King Charles I stepped to his execution on 30 January 1649. The visitor should not fail to note the splendid ceiling painted by Sir Peter Paul Rubens for the unhappy but cultured king

Top favourite with London's millions of visitors and as familiar a sight to Holmes, visiting any of Whitehall's ministries, as it is to us. A trooper of the Queen's Bodyguard of the Royal Horse Guards on guard duty at the Horse Guards, Whitehall. The Horse Guards, a stone building in the Palladian style by William Kent, faces the 'new' War Office

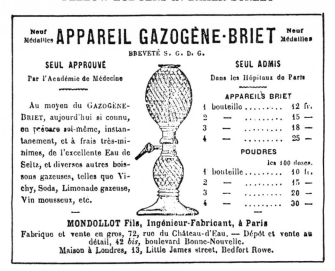

Advertisement for the Mondollot *Gazogène-Briet*, on sale at 13 Little James Street, Bedford Row, from 1878 onwards—the year in which Holmes took up residence in London. It was a *gazogène* of this type which was amongst the more useful accessories at 221B Baker Street

French Republic, the Order of the Legion of Honour, his friendship for France was demonstrated in a delicately flattering way when he purchased a *gazogène*.

Made and marketed by Mondollot fils, *ingénieur-fabricant* in Paris, the *Gazogène-Briet* was on sale at Mondollot's London warehouse, 13 Little James Street, Bedford Row. Even to-day, Bedford Row, because of its close proximity to Gray's Inn, is a favourite street with solicitors, who have only to cross Theobald's (pronounce it 'Tibbles') Road to consult with their chosen barristers in Gray's Inn. It was obviously when consulting some Bedford Row solicitor that Holmes, his eye caught by the glittering nickel-plated-and-wire-bound-glass *gazogènes,* went into Mondollot's and bought what must have been one of the most useful home-adjuncts ever to enter 221B.

In any case, Bedford Row was a mere ten minutes walk from Bart's, where Holmes was studying morbid anatomy and analytical chemistry with equal attention.

The chemical ingenuity of the *Appareil Gazogène-Briet* must have appealed strongly to Holmes's taste; whilst the more human side of him would not, of course, have been indifferent to the virtues of an apparatus which, as the advertisement states, produced excellent Seltzer-water and many other fizzy drinks, such as Vichy, soda, fizzy lemonade, sparkling wine, etc. The year 1878, from which the advertisement of the *gazogène* dates, is, of course, the year in which Holmes began (albeit modestly) to practise in London, so that the *gazogène* may have been brought by him from 24 Montague Street to 221B Baker Street.

CHAPTER 3

The Lighter Side of Holmes's Life

The London of 1878, in which both Holmes and Watson found themselves at the beginnings of their respective professions— Watson, studying for his MD at University College, and Holmes conducting chemical experiments and studying anatomy at Bart's in preparation for a career as 'private consulting detective'—was a London undergoing a change hardly less radical than that which is now sweeping away all but the most revered landmarks.

The Metropolitan Board of Works—predecessor of the London County Council (now renamed the Greater London Council)—had been granted powers almost modern in their authoritarian nature and, like most other bodies 'with the good of the community in mind', they were eager to use them. As the power of compulsory purchase was included in their powers, the Board began to plan 'long-overdue improvements' to London, and to threaten those property-owners understandably reluctant to sell in a forced market, even for the 'common weal'.

Those whom socialist propaganda has misled into thinking that the 'Nobs', a century ago, had it all their own way may not welcome the fact that the principal target for the Board's 'fuehreristically' minatory attitude was His Grace the Duke of Northumberland, on whose huge Tudor mansion at the south-east corner of Trafalgar Square, with vast gardens stretching right down to the Thames, the Board had set its corporate heart. In December 1865, His Grace was served with a compulsory order, and though the snobs of the Metropolitan Board of Works must have been highly gratified at

bove) Trafalgar Square, as Holmes and Watson first knew it. The big curve-fronted
ilding on the right is the world-famous Grand Hotel, opened in June 1880 by the
rdon Hotels Co. With 300 rooms, it was one of the largest as well as the most
urious in Europe. The photograph dates from the age of transition: motor-buses
are the streets with taxi-cabs and horse-drawn vehicles. The Coliseum (1904) is on
e extreme left, but old Morley's Hotel can still be seen behind Nelson's Column.

elow) Trafalgar Square today, little altered, save that South Africa House, behind
lson's Column has replaced Morley's Hotel, and a modern building can be seen, extreme
ht, replacing the Victorian and Charles II buildings at the corner of Villiers Street.
cent cleaning of the surrounding building has contributed to improve the appearance
of the square

having shown their power by serving a writ on a duke, the Duke successfully resisted the order and it was not until 1872 that he 'voluntarily' sold his property to the Board. His change of mind may not, perhaps, have been uninfluenced by the fact that, three years after the first compulsory order had been served on him, a part of Northumberland House, including the ballroom, was destroyed by fire.

In July 1874, the Metropolitan Board of Works, hubristically exalted with their success in having turned a duke out of his ancestral home, invited the public to look over 'its property'. Tickets were issued, and in July 1874, during the last days of old Northumberland House, its huge, echoing corridors and even less small rooms were thronged with the idle, the curious and the malignant.

In London in those days, as in London to-day, property acquired by the misuse of public funds—or, rather, the space on which that property stood—was then released so that 'developers' could make more money than ever the dispossessed property-owners had imagined in their most fantastic dreams.

On the site of Northumberland House and its riverside gardens arose a new street, Northumberland Avenue which, imagined and planned with all the ambition in the world, has remained a dead, forlorn street almost from its inception. Planned to be a street of imposing hotels, with a theatre (The Avenue) at the river end, Northumberland Avenue got its hotels and its theatre, and a grand West End club as well (The Constitutional Club). What its planners did not reckon on was the first World War, which gave government departments even more authoritarian rights over property than had the Metropolitan Board of Works. In the course of that war, the great hotels of Northumberland Avenue—the Grand (1880), the Hotel Métropole (1885) and the Hotel Victoria (1890)—were seized by various government departments, and though released after the war had ended, had been so ruined that recovery was impossible. The owners, Gordon Hotels Ltd, sold the Metropole to the government in 1936 for £300,000: it had been one of the most splendid hotels in the world, and even today, soiled and degraded though it is by the inhuman anonymity of its use, this magnificent building still recalls the noble aspirations of its (perhaps not so noble) entrepreneurs.

At the end of the Hotel Métropole, by the Embankment, there is a round-ended projection on which may be discerned the metal studs which once held some letters in place. The letters have long gone, but the position of the studs will enable you to reconstruct the words, 'Restaurant des Ambassadeurs'. Around this now irretrievably degraded chamber, the cornices of its lofty ceiling exposed by the mindless, pitiless glare of the fluorescent strip-lighting, a piece of railed-in garden still remains. Think back eighty years, or less, and try to imagine the formally-dressed 'patrons' of the Restaurant des Ambassadeurs stepping through the tall French windows on a London night in June, looking across the river, whilst, at their back, the muted violins of the orchestra come softly through

The lavish decoration of the auditorium and proscenium is typical of London's West End theatres at the end of the last century, when impresarios sought to attract 'the better people' as much by the splendour of the surroundings as by the quality of the plays or the progressive elaboration of the scenery. This is the impressive scene within the Princess's Theatre, about 1880

the open windows: *'Le Cygne'*, *'Demande et Réponse'*, *'Eyes that are brightest . . .'*

Looking to their left, they might have seen the velvet-gowned, ospreyed women and the tail-coated men entering the Avenue (later the Playhouse) Theatre across Northumberland Avenue. The theatre is still there: it is now (and has been for years) a studio of the British Broadcasting Corporation, where 'invited audiences' loyally clap everything which appears on the stage before them. The audience is there because someone once told someone else that 'actors acted better before a live audience'—and before a live audience they've had to act ever since.

The Constitutional Club, too, has gone: its premises sold to a developer who has replaced the club by a set of those packing-case offices which do duty for buildings to-day.

We shall see later how Sherlock Holmes came to be intimately associated with Northumberland Avenue—a place of pilgrimage for every ardent Sherlockian, if ever there was one. But let us return for a moment to the expanding, exploding London of Holmes's young days.

From about the mid-century, the itch to rebuild London had seized not only the government but all its subordinate organizations. New streets were either being driven or planned in every part of old and new London. The first really important new street was Victoria Street, connecting Victoria Station with Westminster Abbey, Whitehall and (along Whitehall) Charing Cross and the Strand.

Cutting ruthlessly through a maze of ancient streets, lined with buildings going back to late medieval times (including Caxton's house), Victoria Street not only produced London's first flats, or 'apartments' as they are termed in the USA—modelled on their successful Viennese prototypes—but indicated the pattern that London living was to follow ever more closely over the next century. For these flats—'service flats' they would be called to-day—were being let on long leases in 1866 at £300 a year: a rent to make one pause, seeing that houses in Elm Park Gardens (17 rooms) were being leased as late as 1930 at only £156 a year.

By 1890, in addition to Victoria Street, these important new streets had been cut through London's meandering roads and alleys: Charing Cross Road (1887), Shaftesbury Avenue (1887), Queen Victoria Street (1869-71). As well, the following had been

Old houses, now demolished, in Craig's Court, Whitehall. When Holmes began his career as a private consultant in 1878, Craig's Court was then, and for many years afterwards, the centre of London's private detective business. There were no fewer than six detective agencies operating from this still existing and still old-fashioned court

widened, often to a considerable extent: Piccadilly Circus (the alterations had involved turning the 'Circus' from a circle to a lop-sided square!), Coventry Street (joining Piccadilly Circus with Leicester Square), the Strand (widening begun in 1823 and not yet completed even to-day). Then, most ambitious project of all, came Bazalgette's Embankment stretching from Chelsea to Blackfriars, the extension to the Pool of London having been prevented by what can only be called the irrational prejudice of the Lord Mayor of London and his Common Council.

On these new streets and widened old ones, Elizabethan, Jacobean, Caroline and Georgian buildings were torn down to make way for what, in their day, were as modern, as 'with it' and as tasteless as the edifices which are rising to line the streets to-day.

New hotels—and heaven knows that London was in need of them!—multiplied in a style of expansive comfort unknown to previous generations of hotel-building: the Buckingham Palace Hotel* (1861), the Westminster Palace Hotel* (1866), the Langham (1863), the Inns of Court (1866)—it cost £166,000—the Alexandra, Hyde Park Corner (1863), the Grosvenor (1861), the last-named being part of the 'amenities' connected with Victoria Station, the original laying out of which—it has been altered and added to many times since—cost no less than £675,000. All these hotels established new standards of luxury and paved the way for the ultra-luxurious standards of the hotels of the century's end, when hotel standards reached a peak never attained either before or since.

In all this frenzied building, in which the provision of pleasure (generally speaking) was the dominant motive—pleasure of eating, sleeping, living, and being entertained—restaurants and theatres and music-halls multiplied enormously. And because of the numbers of such places, the competition was at its most vigorous, and so the tendency of prices was to remain at the very economic minimum.

The Globe restaurant, 4-5 Coventry Street, was a place, if not of the very top class, then a good way above the middle. Luncheon at the Globe cost 2s—*five* courses, served between 12 and 2.30 pm. A five-course dinner—almost certainly the same set of dishes, but no matter!—cost 3s. In Previtali's Hotel, in Arundel Place (where the Coventry Street Corner House now stands), you could get a lunch for 8d!—*and* Previtali's and the nearby Mathis (equally inexpensive) provided staff-interpreters to act as guides to foreign visitors who spoke no English.

The theatres and music-halls were equally plentiful and equally competitive, not only in price but also in attractiveness. Old theatres were being rebuilt, new ones rising everywhere; and with this boom in theatre building came several important new approaches to dramatic 'realisation' and presentation.

Perhaps the most important, certainly the most memorable of these new approaches to 'theatre' was to be seen at the Savoy Theatre which opened in 1881, the year in which Holmes and Watson met, with the light opera, *Patience*, in which Gilbert's

---

*The buildings of both—offices now—still survive in, respectively, Buckingham Palace Road and Victoria Street.

topical wit and Sullivan's tuneful airs combined under the imaginative management of D'Oyly Carte to provide London, and eventually the world, with a perennially popular art form. It is impossible that Holmes, one of whose favourite restaurants—Simpson's Divan—was in the Strand, only a few yards from the Savoy Theatre, should not have gone to see the skit on Oscar Wilde and the Aesthetes, at which all London was laughing.

The Strand, in those gas-lit but still brightly lit days, was a street of theatres. Electric light had arrived—the enterprising D'Oyly Carte advertised in his playbills that the Savoy Theatre was illuminated with 'the electric light'—but for all the bars and most of the other places of entertainment, from high-class Irving melodrama at the Lyceum to more down-to-earth corn of the *Married for Money* type at the old Gaiety Theatre, lighting was still by gas.

For all the skill of the cinema illusionist, scene-painting and stage setting have never touched the heights of grandeur, allied with realism of the most impressive kind, that they reached in the Victorian theatre. Such a scenic artist as Hawes Craven (1837-1910), who worked principally for Fechter (Dickens's friend) and Irving, has never been rivalled since. Looking at some of these ambitious scenes and stage sets, one feels that money was counted as no obstacle in the search for the really convincing illusion: Victorian audiences were surely one of the most pampered that the world has ever known!

I turn through the pages of Richard Southern's *The Victorian Theatre** and wonder if even the greatest of the cinema's producers ever commissioned so splendid a scene as that designed by the great William Telbin for Irving's production of *Romeo and Juliet* at the Lyceum in 1882, with Ellen Terry playing Juliet to Irving's Romeo. Holmes, who loved Shakespeare enough to be able to quote him ('The Empty House' and 'Abbey Grange') and knew the Lyceum well (*The Sign of Four*), cannot have missed this superb production, nor in all likelihood those other Irving melodramas, notably the nerve-tingling production of *Macbeth* in 1888, in which, with consummate art, Irving presented blood-and-thunder ham to audiences convinced that they were sitting, reverently enthralled, at the apotheosis of literary and dramatic art. Well, so they were . . . in a way; but it wasn't the way they thought.

*David & Charles, 1970.

In those days, when the theatre, though not the only form of public entertainment by a long way, was by far the principal and most popular, the Strand was London's most theatrical street. On the south side were the Savoy, Terry's, the Strand, the Tivoli Music Hall; on the north, the Adelphi (opened 1806 and rebuilt 1858, 1910 and 1930), outside the stage-door of which the popular actor, William Terriss, was stabbed to death by a disgruntled actor on 16 December 1897; the Vaudeville, the Gaiety, the Olympic (it was in Wych Street, but was connected with the Strand by a long, dark, dirty, smelly and, many feared, an exceedingly dangerous passage). And just at the back of the Strand's north side were the Theatre Royal, Drury Lane—then as much a home of melodrama as the Lyceum—and the Royal Opera House, Covent Garden.

The Lyceum, which has been a Mecca-owned dance-hall for several years now, has a curious connection with Holmes, quite apart from any plays that he saw there. The first Lyceum, a concert-hall, was built by Dr Samuel Arnold, great-grandfather of Edgar Allan Poe, creator of that fictional detective, the Chevalier C. Auguste Dupin, whom Holmes affected to despise—'Now, in my opinion, Dupin was a very inferior fellow . . .'—but whose reasoning, as the late William Baring-Gould has pointed out, Holmes was not too proud to adopt. The original Lyceum was destroyed by fire, in 1834, and immediately rebuilt in its present form by S. Beazley, the architect. Just before the first World War, the interior was entirely rebuilt, though the 1834 façade was, for understandably sentimental reasons, retained unaltered. Shabby though the exterior is today, it is still the Lyceum to which the Victorians, Holmes and Watson amongst them, flocked during three-quarters of a century.

Of the theatres, concert-halls and music halls extant and doing vigorous and enthusiastically-supported business in Holmes's day, the Canon mentions only six: the Allegro (almost certainly Watson's whimsical 'pseudonym' for the Gaiety); Covent Garden where, in, nearby Covent Garden Market, on Tuesday, 27 December 1887, Holmes recovered, from the crop of a fat goose left over from the Christmas trade, the missing blue carbuncle of the Countess of Morcar, valued at £20,000. Then the Canon mentions the Haymarket Theatre, properly the Theatre Royal, Haymarket, originally built to the designs of Nash and opened on American Independence

Day, 4 July 1821. The Haymarket, at which Lily Langtry, intimate friend of Albert, Prince of Wales (afterwards King Edward VII) made her theatrical début, was entirely rebuilt internally in 1907, but, as in the case of the Lyceum, the original classical façade was retained for reasons of sentiment. It is this front which is still familiar to London theatregoers today.

The Canon also mentions both those famous—one surviving, one vanished—'homes of music': the Albert Hall and St James's Hall. The latter was a favourite of Holmes's, not only because it was handy—on the 'Atlas' green bus from Baker Street, fare: 1d—but also because it was here that he could enjoy the playing of his favourite violinist, Wilma Norman-Neruda, afterwards Lady Hallé. If you remember, halfway through the case of 'A Study in Scarlet', Holmes proposes to Watson a break from labour for refreshment, both of body and of mind: 'And now for lunch, and then for Norman-Neruda. Her attack and her bowing are splendid, what's that little thing of Chopin's she plays so magnificently: Tra-la-la-lira-lira-lay'.

The St James's Hall, opened in April 1858 at a cost of £60,000, was demolished in 1904 to make way for the present Piccadilly Hotel, built on a site extending from Piccadilly in the south to Regent Street Quadrant in the north, between 1905 and 1908. The St James's Restaurant, adjacent to and part of St James's Hall, was of an elegance not to be found today; and St James's Hall, with its noble repertoires, drew all in London and the provinces who appreciated the best in music presented under the baton of the best of conductors. Wilma Norman-Neruda, probably the most *appreciated* of all artists—she was named, by royal warrant, 'Violinist in Ordinary to Her Majesty'—was as popular with the masses as she was with the connoisseurs, and a villa in the South of France, subscribed for by the aristocracy and landed gentry of England (with a lead from many members of the royal family, headed by the Queen and the Prince of Wales), was not amongst the principal of Madame Norman-Neruda's gains from her extraordinary mastery of the violin.

It is true that experienced and not-so-experienced musicians have been puzzled by Holmes's reference to 'that little thing of Chopin's she plays so magnificently: Tra-la-la-lira-lira-lay'—which sounds, at first hearing, more like Percy Quilter at his most rustic than anything which issued from Chopin. The most plausible explanation of the quote is that Watson was no musician, and that what he 'quoted' in this context ought not to have any bearing on Holmes's musical knowledge. The general opinion is that the 'Tra-la-la-lira-lira-lay' is Watson's, not Chopin's or Holmes's.

Another age than that of the Edwardian might have preserved the St James's Hall as it preserved the Albert Hall; but the Albert Hall has always been, since its opening by Queen Victoria in 1871, regarded as something sacrosanct. This is possibly because of its name, possibly because of the deep personal interest that Queen Victoria took in its design and building, or possibly because, to replace the Albert Hall with a building holding the same number of people—12,000—would cost too much for even the quick-buck-chasing 'developers' of today. And where else would they sing *Hiawatha*?

That Holmes visited the Albert Hall is made clear from a reference in 'The Adventures of the Retired Colourman' (the case extended from Thursday, 28 July to Saturday, 30 July 1898). He also had need to visit the royal borough of Kensington—for instance, before having gone to Odessa in the case of the Trepoff murder, he would have had to call in at the Imperial Russian Embassy in Chesham Place (moving later to Kensington Palace Gardens), for both a general briefing on the Trepoff situation and, naturally, to have his British passport *visé* by the Russian consular officials.

To combine a visit to the Russian Embassy with an evening's pleasure at the Albert Hall (followed by a shilling's worth of hansom cab from Kensington Road to Baker Street) would have seemed to Holmes a most reasonable arrangement. Or, instead of taking a hansom, he could have cut across the Park by the Round Pond and called on Watson, after the doctor, recovered from the wound received at Maiwand, had purchased a small practice in Paddington. (The dates are helpful: Watson, after his first marriage to Miss Constance Adams of San Francisco on 1 November 1886, almost certainly bought his Paddington practice in the same month, the very month in which Holmes, summoned to Odessa, would have had to call in at the Russian Embassy. Holmes would not even have had to walk across the Park to see Watson: he could have continued up Kensington Palace Gardens to Notting Hill, and walked through Sussex Square or one of the other Bayswater squares to

Watson's house, which was in the vicinity of Paddington Station.)

Where the Palladium now stands, was until 1910, Hengler's Circus, home of dashing steeds, equestriennes, clowns and the tight-wire artistes. The circus comes into the Canon in 'The Case of the Veiled Lodger', a case of jealousy and revenge more emotionally charged than the majority of Holmes's cases. One may say that this case brought Holmes into contact with the world of the circus, but may not it have been the other way around? Whether walking from Montague Street or Baker Street (or taking hansom or four-wheeler), the distance to Hengler's Circus, in Argyll Street, Oxford Circus, would have been roughly the same, a matter of minutes. Hengler's was so near to wherever Holmes's London address may have been that it seems unlikely that the two men did not visit it, and perhaps it was here that the circus folk got to know of both the great skill and the great compassion of the Sleuth of Baker Street.

But for all the circuses and music-halls and *cafés concerts* ('The Coal Hole' in the Strand was one of the most famous, Evans's Rooms in Covent Garden having passed their prime), it is clear that Holmes's tastes were, if not altogether 'highbrow', then certainly a cut above the sentimental slush or the near-the-knuckle vulgarity of such places as Collins's, the Oxford, the Canterbury, the St George's, the Shoreditch and other famous music-halls. To Ley-bourne, the Great Vance, Nelly Farren, Albert Chevalier, Holmes prefers Carina at the Albert Hall, Norman-Neruda at the St James's Hall, and the De Reskes, Polish brothers whose singing fame, other-wise forgotten, is commemorated in the name of a popular brand of British cigarette. The De Reskes were as much favourites with King Edward VII as Norman-Neruda had been with Queen Victoria. Holmes liked them all.

As there are references to 'the opera' in both *The Hound of the Baskervilles* and 'The Case of The Red Circle', it is clear that the musically-inclined and—may we say it?—socially-conscious Holmes attended the opera which, in those days in London, was inferior to none in the world.

Every foreign artist of note came, as a matter of course, to London: actors and actresses to the Haymarket or the St James's, great singers to the Royal Opera House, Albert Hall or the concert-rooms—vast auditoria, decorated and furnished with the utmost luxury—of the big hotels which sprang up in London after 1860.

In addition, the drawing-rooms of great houses were small, but not so *very* small theatres in themselves, and, even as late as 1930, many of the old Town houses of the nobility and other aristocracy were still maintained in the style which had been the unremarkably normal in the 1880s. The private recital at Lady Combermere's London house, at which the 'divine' but unpunctual Sarah Bernhardt kept the high-class audience waiting for an hour is remarkable only for Sarah's discourtesy and her ability to get away with it—to the great indignation of Lady Frederick Cavendish, who complained to a friend:

> London has gone mad over the principal actress in the Comédie Française who are here: Sarah Bernhardt, a woman of notorious character. Not content with being run after on the stage, this woman is asked to respectable people's houses to act, and even to luncheon and dinner, and all the world goes. It is an outrageous scandal!

Later, Sarah was to claim that her son, Maurice, was not by the Prince de Ligne—as people had supposed, and she had claimed—but by the Duke of Clarence, eldest son of the Prince of Wales, afterwards King Edward VII. The Prince de Ligne and the Duke of Clarence had been born in the same year, 1864, and it is *just* possible that Sarah had mistaken the fathers whilst remembering the year. It is more than likely that Holmes, who was offered a knighthood (it was declined) in the year in which the Prince of Wales became King, was called in, with the utmost discretion, in an affair which was connected with this possible liaison between Sarah Bernhardt and the heir-but-one to the throne of Great Britain and Ireland and the Empire of India. If the late William Baring-Gould's surmises are correct, Holmes had already been of inestimable service to the Prince of Wales, and if Holmes had also served the Prince's son, Albert Victor, Duke of Clarence, the Prince—now King—would have been eager to reward Holmes. But Holmes (according to Baring-Gould) had conceived an aversion for the King as Prince of Wales, and was in no mind to accept honours from him.

But, despite scandal, or perhaps because of it, Sarah Bernhardt was the rage of London from her first visit here in 1879, when she was greeted at Folkestone by Oscar Wilde with a big sheaf of arum and madonna lilies in his arms. Oscar, then at the apotheosis of his fame, or notoriety, as the Apostle of the Utterly-Utter, spread the lilies upon the ground, inviting Sarah (who loved flowers and respected the money paid out for them) to tread the lilies beneath her 'incomparable' feet. Then crying 'Vive Bernhardt!', Oscar led the crowd in the salutation until the Folkestonians of 1879 had more or less approximated to the French.

Watson's use of the name, 'Lord Cantlemere', in 'The Adventure of the Mazarin Stone' is fairly strong evidence that Holmes (with, perhaps, Watson) was at Lady Combermere's 'At Home' when Sarah Bernhardt kept her audience waiting an hour. But whether Holmes was or was not present in Berkeley Square on that memorable occasion, he must have seen Sarah on 4 June 1879, when she electrified London—there is no other word for it—in *Phèdre en toute sa fureur*. The English might have read, rather haltingly, no doubt, Racine's play of incestuous lust, but to hear the super-intelligent and super-sexual Bernhardt scream her complaint to the gods who have 'lit the fatal blaze in my loins' blood' was an experience that no London theatre-goer could have failed to find both unprecedented and unique. A contemporary critic remarks on the silence with which the audience left the Gaiety Theatre on that memorable night. One understands the silence . . .

Holmes, it is clear, was not the misogynist that Watson thought him, for all that the Sleuth of Baker Street only sleuthed women in the way of business and never in that of pleasure. Holmes, alas, had a highly specialised taste in women; he liked them to be both sexually attractive *and* intelligent—which explains the infrequency of his praise for women and the fact that he never married. It also accounts, at least in part, for the fact that the woman who most attracted him ('To Sherlock Holmes', Watson wrote, 'she is always *the* woman. I have seldom heard him mention her under any other name. In his eyes she eclipses and predominates the whole of her sex . . .') was, as Watson honestly but tactlessly recalled, 'of dubious and questionable memory'. But for all that Irene Adler was an 'adventuress'—a Victorian euphemism for a well-paid strumpet—Holmes responded to her mind, to her quick wit, to her undeniable intelligence. He could, and did, forgive her everything, this cold, seemingly austere man, because she had a brain and used it—even to Holmes's undoing.

For the same reason, he must have liked and liked to see Sarah Bernhardt. Here he had his wish granted, for though Irene Adler

('*The* Woman') had retired from the operatic stage after her last tremendous triumph as prima donna at the Imperial Opera, Warsaw, Sarah was still active, and would remain so until her death thirty-four years later in 1923.

Since that first electrifying appearance in *Phèdre*, Bernhardt had captured London; and London still talked of her, even that part of the capital which did not have either the inclination or the ability to go to Paris (first-class return from Victoria, £2 12s 6d). They looked forward to her return, but when it came, it was in exceptional circumstances which must surely be echoed in Watson's tactful editing of the case of 'A Scandal in Bohemia'. Conceiving a violent passion for Aristides ('Jacques') Damala, a young attaché of the Greek Legation in Paris, who had already been asked, as a *persona non grata*, to remove himself from France, Sarah decided to marry him. As she was a Roman Catholic and Damala Greek Orthodox, and no Papal licence was forthcoming for this religiously-mixed marriage, the forty-year-old actress and the twenty-nine-year-old 'diplomatic Apollo' caught the fastest train from Naples, where Sarah was playing, and hurried to London where, on 4 April at St Andrew's Church, Wells Street, Oxford Street, they were married.

It cannot be a coincidence that Irene Adler, who so resembled Sarah Bernhardt in both intelligence and freedom of morals, should have been married in just such a whirlwind way to Godfrey Norton at St Monica's Church (perhaps St Saviour's, at the junction of Clifton Gardens and Warrington Crescent). The likeness is too striking, even to the matter of the special licence and the great disparity in ages between the bride and her young husband.

Immediately after her marriage, Sarah returned to France, but a few months later she came back to London, to greater triumphs than before. This time, with her new husband playing the male lead, she aroused even wilder enthusiasm as *La Dame aux Camélias*: the Prince and Princess of Wales attended the first night, and afterwards went to the Green Room to congratulate Sarah. Beautiful Princess Alexandra put her arms around the actress and, weeping, said, 'Oh, Madame, I am so happy to find you still alive after that last act!'

Bernhardt's *Theodora*, in which she played the sixth-century harlot-empress of Byzantium, was a smash hit in both Paris and

London, in which latter city it ran for a hundred nights, a long run for those days.

We may imagine that Holmes saw all of Bernhardt's plays, the successes and the flops (they were few, but there were some).

But it is clear that when Holmes went out to seek relaxation from problem-solving, it was to *hear* rather than *see*. An actor himself— no master of disguise, as was Holmes, could have changed appearance and character without having mastered all the skills of acting —even the best play must have seemed to Holmes something in the nature of a busman's holiday; and though it is true that, as Watson reports, he was a master-musician, to hear another play is not as boring to a musician as seeing another act is to an actor. It was to the many first-rate concert-halls of the day that Holmes went to be refreshed after a day's honest man-hunting.

We have seen that amongst his favourites was the Czech violinist, Wilma Norman-Neruda. Not less popular with Holmes was the Spanish violinist, Pablo Sarasate, whom, you may recall, Holmes went to hear at the St James's Hall as a 'breather', between acts in the case of 'The Red-Headed League'.

Holmes, it will be recalled, wrote on music as well as played it; he was a musicologist as well as an accomplished musician. Doubt has been cast, not merely on Holmes's authorship but on the very existence of his monograph on the 'Polyphonic Motets of Lassus',* a work which, says Watson, 'is said by experts to be the last word on the subject'. However, there is little doubt that the work was, as Watson said, printed for private circulation, and the reason why the monograph is not better known or conveniently available is that it was printed for no less a patron of Holmes's skill than Queen Victoria herself.

Mr. Trevor H. Hall, in his *Sherlock Holmes; Ten Literary Studies* (Duckworth, 1969) makes out a strong case for the supposition that Queen Victoria—like most other members of the Royal Family, over several generations, a lover of music and of musicians—'after a lifetime of diligent study . . . would need only to seek instruction in regard to a musical subject upon which printed sources were incomplete and original research was needed'. The subject, Mr Hall asserts, was Lassus, as a famous, indeed, the most famous composer

---

*This work, which has been hotly debated in Sherlockian circles, is examined in my *In the Footsteps of Sherlock Holmes*.—M.H.

of motets in the sixteenth century. That Orlando Lassus was also a diplomat engaged on the most secret errands may have first attracted Holmes's notice to him, whilst the finding of a dossier of Lassus's diplomatic reports in the great clearing-out of Windsor Castle, ordered and seen to be carried through by the Prince Consort, may first have called the Queen's attention to the merits and mystery of the composer.

The question that I now ask, and that Mr Hall has not raised, is this: was Holmes's name first brought to Her Majesty's attention as a musicologist (with a special interest in Lassus, perhaps?) or as a detective?

Her Majesty's practical Hanoverian mind may well have appreciated the advantages of patronising a young man of good reputation who was both musicologist *and* outstandingly successful detective. That Holmes was decidedly odd, sometimes to the point of eccentricity, would not have worried the Queen: there had been, and were still, too many oddities in her own family for the presence of one more eccentric at Windsor or Buckingham Palace to have perturbed her.

But why should Holmes's skill as a detective have attracted her to him? Well, in the first place, Holmes had not only been of service in hushing up some scandals in the British royal family, he had also helped, as we have seen, German and Scandinavian royalty to a happier frame of mind. The royalty of those days were all connected, not only by blood and marriage but also—a fact too easily overlooked—by a voluminous, completely holograph personal correspondence, whose writing alone would take all a person's work and leisure time in these less energetic days. What Holmes had done for Germany and Scandinavia would have been kept no secret from the Queen, whose daughter had been German Empress and whose son was married to a princess of Denmark.

But there was a much more personal reason for the Queen's interest in Holmes—her known and recorded interest in Jack the Ripper. This is no place to air a theory of mine as to the identity of this sadistic killer—I have told the full story in another place.* But it is a matter of public record that the Queen was not only indignant at the failure of Sir Charles Warren and his Metropolitan Police to find the murderer, but wrote her own suggestions to him

*Clarence, by Michael Harrison; W. H. Allen.

and to the newspapers. Rarely can *The Times* have received so distinguished a 'Sir . . . ' letter!

It is inconceivable that the Queen, meddling in this affair of the Ripper with even more gusto than she meddled, to Gladstone's irritation, in affairs of state, should not have commanded the presence of the one man with whom she could have discussed the case intelligently, constructively and—important, this—from a point-of-view necessarily *not* that of the hide-bound, convention-ridden police; especially a police at whose head was a gentlemanly retired military officer of the very old school.

Mr Baring-Gould says that Holmes solved the Ripper murder; but Holmes's reasoning wasn't mine. However, Holmes, unlike Sir Charles Warren, *did* something, and that was what the Queen had asked for.

Queen Victoria with her eldest daughter, the Empress Frederick of Germany. A keen student of contemporary criminology, she even wrote to *The Times* on the subject of Jack the Ripper—Queen Victoria's interest in Holmes was of a more personal nature : there was hardly a royal family in Europe to which he had not been of service

Once the heart of a world-empire and still the heart of a world-common-wealth: Parliament Square, Westminster, hardly changed since its last big alteration in 1900, when King Street was covered by the completion of the government block begun in 1862. This aerial shot shows the House of Commons, near right, King Henry VII's Chapel, near left; St Margaret's, Westminster, middle left amongst the trees and, fronting Parliament Street and Whitehall, upper left and right, various Ministries

Watson tells us that Holmes was hard at work trying to finish his monograph on the Polyphonic Motets of Lassus when the affair of the Bruce-Partington plans cropped up, and hurriedly returned to his interrupted writing as soon as this case had been satisfactorily disposed of. Mr Trevor Hall says of the Bruce-Partington affair (in which young Cadogan West was killed) that Holmes obviously regarded it as of much less importance than the writing of the monograph. What Mr Hall has overlooked is that, in this case—'It's a vital international problem that you have to solve . . . In all your career you have never had so great a chance of serving your country'.—Holmes was using his peculiar skills at the highest level of state policy: summoned to help by government, and serving the Queen far more importantly than in pleasing her with a monograph on a long-dead composer.

In rewarding him, Her Majesty's highly personal gift acknowledged both his services to the Crown: the matter of the Bruce-Partington plans and the matter of the monograph on Lassus.

The Queen was at Windsor in the late November of 1895 when a closed carriage, discreetly painted in the sober maroon with scarlet lining of the royal colours, pulled up, in a pea-souper fog, outside 221B, and a messenger from the Lord Chamberlain's department gave a heavily sealed envelope to 'our boy in buttons'.

'For Mr Sherlock Holmes', said the messenger. It was a command to attend upon the Royal Person at Her Court at Windsor. It named a day, and Holmes, never quite punctual, leapt into a hansom with his usual cry of 'Paddington—the slope entrance. Half-a-sovereign for yourself if you can catch the 9.15'. They made it and the cabby earned his half-sovereign.

Watson tells us what happened.

'. . . Some weeks afterwards I learned incidentally that my friend spent a day at Windsor, whence he returned with a remarkably fine emerald tie-pin. When I asked him if he had bought it, he answered that it was a present from a certain gracious lady in whose interests he had been fortunate enough to carry out a small commission'. The assiduity with which he tackled that monograph is explained; the pin—a tie-pin was a favourite present with the royalty of those more spacious days—probably came from R. S. Garrard & Co, Crown Jewellers and Goldsmiths, of 25 Haymarket, S.W. Most of the royal tie-pins came from Garrard's or Carrington & Co, of 130 Regent Street. Carrington's are still in Regent Street, and Garrard's are now their near neighbours.

On one musical point—or, rather, a matter of musical taste—

Gloucester Road Station, on the District (Underground) Line.
It was along the tunnel at Gloucester Road that Holmes and
Watson went to find out where the evil Hugo Oberstein had
flung the body of young Cadogan West on to a passing
train in 'The Affair of The Bruce-Partington Plans'

Holmes, as obstinate in his way as was the Queen in hers, must
have agreed to differ with his august hostess over the China tea
and the thin bread-and-butter in one of the smaller drawing-rooms
at Windsor. That point was Wagner.

In the case of 'The Red Circle', Watson leaves on record that
Holmes attended a Wagner night at Covent Garden, and Watson's

implication is that Holmes thoroughly enjoyed himself. But the Queen's view of the German composer was not Holmes's: '. . . that queer man, Richard Wagner, who wrote such extraordinary music —surely Germany was a little mad about him (*ie, mad to give him such respect*)'.

But the music-loving Queen—even six years before her death (she was then seventy-six, and deaf) she was still polishing her music under the leading masters of the day—must have agreed with her detective friend on most other musical points: the splendid singing of the De Reske brothers in Meyerbeer's *Les Huguenots* (*The Hound of the Baskervilles*), Sarasate, Carina, whom Holmes heard at the Albert Hall, and of course, Norman-Neruda.

In a London which provided in lavish degree, as never before or since, first-class entertainment on the light, middle-level and heavy-weight strata, there was plenty of less highbrow entertainment for Holmes and Watson, as a contrast to Carina at the Albert Hall or Wagner at Covent Garden. At the Alhambra and the Empire in Leicester Square they could see anything from red-nosed comedy to performing dogs, and at the Empire they could see, too, that promenade of strumpets which was regarded by many as the Empire's principal (as it was its permanent) business

It was against the Empire—or, more particularly, the harlots of the Empire promenade and those of the nearby Leicester Lounge, down whose two flights of brass-edged stairs the drunk and the obstreperous were flung straight on to the pavement of Leicester Square—that a malignant do-gooder of the last century, Mrs Ormiston Chant, paraded with banners which shouted: 'SAVE OUR LADS FROM SIN!'

Fearful of this moral harpy, the management of the Empire at last gave in to the cry which has always had power to arouse the fighting spirit of wowsers—'Interfere with the pleasure of others!'—and caused screens to be erected between the auditorium and the promenade: the famous (or notorious, depending how you were made) Empire Gallery.

A number of young men, outraged by this pitiable surrender to wowser opinion, stormed the Empire and by main force tore down the offending screens to the cheers of both the whores and the audience alike. It is not the least praiseworthy act of the late Sir Winston Churchill that he assisted, some even say led, this assault on a gross interference with the rights of man.

The old Leicester Lounge had passed its prime as I recall it, just before it was absorbed, in 1926, into the neighbouring drapery store of Stagg & Russell. But if the brass-and-mahogany and potted palm splendour of 'the Lounge' had passed its prime, what shall I say of the painted harridans who hung about, nursing their gin-and-Its, for all the world as though it were still 1879.

The Leicester Lounge went to 1926; not, after all, because of Mrs Ormiston Chant, but because there was more profit selling women's underwear than selling beer and 8d-a-tot whisky. In the following year, the Empire went, too, but far more spectacularly than did the now dingy old Leicester Lounge. On the evening of 21 January 1927, the final curtain was rung down on one of the Empire's most successful shows: *Lady Be Good*, in which the ever-popular Fred and (the late) Adèle Astaire enchanted London with their singing and dancing. Adèle went on to marry a son of the Duke of Devonshire; Fred, as I write this, is happily still with us, and still acting and dancing.

It was a memorable and sentimental occasion. I was there, but it is no modesty which makes me assert that I was not the most famous guest that night: it was the Prince of Wales, now Duke of Windsor. What made the last night so unusually depressing was the realisation that the great theatre was only forty years old. Opened in November 1887, it was now closing within ten months of its fortieth birthday, and several older members of our party could remember the first night. The implications of this hurry to build, tear down and build again were not lost on many that night.

In the decade after Holmes had 'set up his plate' (or 'shingle', as the Americans say) in Baker Street, more theatres were built in London than in any other decade, before or since. Many were in connection with the two new streets leading, one into Piccadilly Circus and the other into Trafalgar Square, but the new theatres in Shaftesbury Avenue and Charing Cross Road inspired the owners of many less central theatres—for instance, the Novelty (later Kingsway, now vanished) Theatre, on the north side of Great Queen Street. It was built by Penley, the comedian. Another rebuilding of the 1880s was the Avenue Theatre, opened in 1882 as part of the Northumberland Avenue development. The collapse of the steel-and-glass roof of Charing Cross Station smashed the theatre completely; compensation of £30,000 was paid by the South Eastern & Chatham Railway Company, and the rebuilt theatre, now named The Playhouse—still its name—was re-opened by the actor-manager, Cyril Maude who had been its first manager in 1882.

Several of the London theatres, new or rebuilt, of the 1880s are still with us: the Comedy Theatre, Panton Street, the Garrick Theatre (1889), the Duke of York's (1889), the Apollo, the Globe, the Queen's —all 1887-1890. The Shaftesbury Theatre, on the south side of Shaftesbury Avenue, also dates from this period; opened in October 1888, it was hit by bombs in 1940 and completely demolished in an air raid in the following year. It was a 'lucky' theatre, specialising in long runs, amongst them two 'hit' musical comedies, *The Belle of New York* (1898) and *The Arcadians* (1909) and a thriller, *The Sorrows of Satan*, in the film version of which I first saw the hooded-eyed Ricardo Cortez, many, many years ago.

The 'continental' cafés of London—and I would say that, in proportion, there were even more foreigners in the capital then than there are today; certainly there were far more foreigners engaged in business—cannot be considered apart from the theatres and other places of entertainment. For 'dinner-and-theatre' or 'theatre-and-supper' was the popular night-out 'package deal' of late Victorian London's leisure hours, and restaurateurs and theatre-managers worked, instinctively if not actually, in the closest co-operation.

The link between them was strengthened by the fact that the new streets—Shaftesbury Avenue, Charing Cross Road, Northumberland Avenue and the Embankment—were closely connected with the building of the hotels and cafés which had arisen along the new streets.

In Piccadilly Circus, there were the Criterion Hotel, Restaurant and bars (1873) which, with its attached Criterion Theatre (1874), made up its own 'package deal'. Across the way, in the Circus greatly enlarged (and squared off) in 1879-80, were the rebuilt Pavilion Music Hall (1881) with its four external and three internal bars, the famous Café Monico, founded by two young Swiss in 1879. There were the already mentioned Globe Restaurant, Previtali's, the Mathis Hotel, the famous Florence (corner of Rupert Street and Coventry Street) and Pinoli's, well-known for its Masonic dinners, in Wardour Street.

Amongst the more distinguished patrons of the Florence's two-

A restaurant that Holmes and Watson knew well, and still—
though rebuilt and much changed—doing good business on the
same site. Founded by Monsieur Nichol in 1865 in Glasshouse
Street and afterwards extended to Regent Street, the Café Royal,
in Holmes's younger days, was of a decidedly free-and-easy
character. It was outside the Café Royal in 1902 that Holmes was
bested by two accomplices of Baron Adalbert Gruner, a fact
which did not influence Holmes against the famous Café

shilling, five-course dinners—they were still only three shillings on
the outbreak of World War II—was Oscar Wilde.

In Regent Street's Quadrant was the Café Royal, a favourite with Sherlock Holmes. Opened in 1865 by a French immigrant, Monsieur Nichol (it is his 'N', not Napoleon's, which enters into so much of the decoration of the Café Royal, though how old Nichol got the imperial crown which tops the 'N', no one knows!), the Café Royal, as I remember it, was very different from the new Café Royal which arose on the rebuilding of 1923, and even *that* new Café Royal was still a homely place compared with the newest of Café Royals, still however, doing expense-account business on the old pitch. In the last century, when Holmes and Watson visited the Café Royal, it was a very French café-restaurant indeed, with red-plush-upholstered banquettes against the lavishly mirrored walls, and Madame Nichol, who managed the Café Royal after her husband's death in 1897, sitting, in true French *patronne* fashion, in her little glass-walled desk, taking the money and saying good-bye to the customers.

I should like to stop a little while in my listing of the cafés and and café-restaurants of Holmes's day to consider a reason which may have taken Holmes to the Café Royal at about the time of Monsieur Nichol's death. We know that Holmes and Watson were in the café in 1895, for that was the time at which he solved the mystery of the Bruce-Partington plans and explained the killing of young Cadogan West. It is a curious fact to reflect upon, but Holmes and Watson could not have frequented the Café Royal without having seen the exhibitionistic Oscar Wilde and heard his all-overpowering voice as he lectured to his cronies in the corner by the Glasshouse Street entrance. But *did* Holmes and Watson frequent the Café Royal? It is significant that though Simpson's Café Divan is mentioned early in the Canon in connection with 'The Case of the Dying Detective' (Saturday, 19 November 1889 or shortly before), the Café Royal is not mentioned until the case of 'The Bruce-Partington Plans' (Thursday, 21 November to Saturday, 23 November 1895).

Now it was only shortly before this case that Oscar Wilde, having lost his libel action against the Marquess of Queensbury, was arrested, tried and sentenced to two years' imprisonment with hard labour at Reading Gaol. Lord Alfred Douglas went abroad, and the other members of the Oscar-Wilde-Café-Royal set went their several discreet ways. The silence in the Café Royal must have been grateful to ears compelled to listen most nights of the week to Oscar's wit and his friends' sycophantic titters.

It looks, then, as though Holmes decided to visit—re-visit is more probably correct—the Café Royal, now that the Wilde set had vanished. Monsieur and Madame Nichol must have been glad to see that the departure of their 'famous' customers had not ruined their trade. And, knowing who Holmes was, Nichol must have consulted him about the mystery of the dead night-watchman, Monsieur Martin—a name that Watson used when hunting pseudonyms for use in both the case of 'The Gloria Scott' and that of 'The Dancing Men'—respectively, Lieutenant Martin and Inspector Martin.

The year was 1897, and Martin's death was as mysterious as any described by Watson in the Canon. Without, as they say, an enemy in the world—though which of us can really know that?—poor Martin, going the rounds, testing windows and doors, was shot by an intruder whose motives were as mysterious as the death of the man he caused. We cannot, naturally, say that Holmes did *not* solve this murder-mystery, but, if he did the solution was never made public. What heightened the mystery was that Monsieur Nichol, though only a comparatively young man, died shortly afterwards.

And now back to some more of the cafés which made life so pleasant in the world of Holmes's earlier days.

In Regent Street's Quadrant was also Oddenino's Hotel and Restaurant, the bar of which—they called it the Gambrinus, after a mythological German sprite, traditionally a sort of German Bacchus —had been started by a German. Across the Circus, in Leicester Square, cleaned up after 1874 by the generosity of a buck-chasing celebrity of the day named 'Baron' Albert Grant, were some of London's most famous cafés: the Cavour (later the Café Anglais), under the management of Monsieur Philippe, was the best-known and most popular with the cosmopolitan set, but the Café de l'Europe, on the south-east corner of Leicester Place as it joins Leicester Square, was popular, too. Common (British) opinion credited these two well-frequented cafés of decidedly foreign flavour with being the haunts of anarchists and other subversive types. One feels that common opinion had something, at least, to go on. At the corner of Green Street (now Irving Street) and the Square was Hogarth's old house—he settled here in 1735—which later became the very foreign Sablonnier Hotel, and was pulled down in 1870. Holmes would hardly have visited it; he was only sixteen when it was demolished and Archbishop Tenison's School erected on the site, but he would have known the Hotel de Provence, at the corner of Bear Street and the Square, to which the Sablonnier's more obstinately foreign clientèle moved. The Hotel de Provence lasted until 1919, when it was acquired by the catering firm of R. & E. Jones Ltd, itself now absorbed in one of the big 'chains'.

Of course, it was Holmes's intense interest in human beings and, in particular, his need to move professionally at levels far beneath that of the 'Upper Ten', which made him so familiar with the less and least fashionable cafés and restaurants of London. But it was not poverty which kept him away from the smart places, any more than it could have been diffidence. There are two references to Claridge's Hotel in the Canon, though both 'The Problem of Thor Bridge': 4-5 October 1900 and *His Last Bow*: 2 August 1914, date from after 1895, the year in which Mrs Claridge, widow of the retired butler, again rebuilt the hotel which, beginning as Mivart's in 1808 and a favourite with the Regency bucks, had been bought by Claridge in mid-century. But there is no need to suppose that Holmes did not know the original Claridge's as well as he knew the rebuilt premises, which still stand—perhaps London's most favoured hotel—at the corner of Brook Street and Davies Street.

There are other 'superior' places of refreshment mentioned in the Canon: the Grosvenor Hotel (1861) by Victoria Station, an establishment so moral that when Cora Pearl, 'the adventuress', and her current lover Prince Napoleon ('Plon-Plon') arrived as refugees from the collapse of the Second Empire, the hotel management refused to admit them; the 'Cosmopolitan' (almost certainly the top-notching Hotel Métropole in Northumberland Avenue); the Charing Cross Hotel (opened 15 May 1865), one of the first of London's major hotels and still, despite nationalisation, an hotel of the absolutely first class; the Langham, opened 12 June 1863, after a visit from the Prince of Wales, and visited by two thousand people on opening day because of its unprecedented magnificence; the 'Dacre' (Watsonian for the Windsor Hotel, Victoria Street, because it stands on the Dacre Estate); the St Pancras Hotel, correctly the Midland Hotel at St Pancras Station, and one of the great railway termini hotels which once rivalled in cuisine, service and luxurious accommodation the best hotels in the world. Designed by Sir Gilbert Scott and erected at a cost of £500,000, the hotel was opened on 5 May 1873. It was closed down in 1935, so that the railway company could use its palatial rooms as offices. Under 'British Rail' management, dirt and neglect have removed even its fine outer appearance.

The 'Mexborough Hotel' referred to in *The Hound of the Baskervilles*, I have been unable to trace; the Northumberland Hotel, from the same case, is still doing business (though not as an hotel) under the new name of The Sherlock Holmes, but I shall deal with this in a later chapter.

The 'Carlton', referred to in the case of 'The Greek Interpreter' (Wednesday, 12 September 1888) cannot be the splendid hotel and restaurant, and notably the famous Carlton Grill, which stood at the corner of Haymarket and Pall Mall until destroyed to make way for what someone in the New Zealand Government was persuaded was an elegant structure. That Carlton was built between 1897 and 1899, and cannot thus have been the 'Carlton' referred to in a case datable to 1888. Watson's 'Carlton' may, however, have been the old-fashioned but luxurious Garland's Hotel, destroyed in World War II, which lay only the width of the Haymarket from the Carlton.

CHAPTER 4

Sherlock on the Royal Round

Until 1914, London had many palaces, though they were not always called by that name. London still has several, even many palaces, but not a hand-count are inhabited by members of the royal family. And as for all those other palaces that London knew until the outbreak of the first World War—the palaces of the aristocracy, which rivalled and often outshone the splendours of the royal homes—only one or two are still private residences.

One is used to seeing the gilded 'glass coach' of the Sovereign, with its escort of Yeomen of the Guard, making its ponderous and dignified way to and from the opening of Parliament; and every year the same type of picturesque vehicle, in all the impressiveness of gilded baroque, takes the Lord Mayor of London from and to the Mansion House.

Up to the outbreak of the first World War, every aristocratic family had such a coach; many had far more than one such vehicle, their door-panels blazing with the armorial achievements of the family, their hammercloths bearing the same heraldic patterns, their bodywork painted in the livery colours of the family, enriched with gold.

In many families, these old vehicles—the state coaches of the formal occasion, in which they went to Court, called on their Sovereign, drove to this important event and that—still stand in the coach-houses of their country estates: there are no garages in London roomy enough to hold such space-consuming relics.

But in May 1908, for the State visit of the President of France,

King Edward VII riding in the State Coach to open the Parliament of 1903, the ye[?]
in which Holmes retired to his books and his bee-keeping at Cuckmere Haven, f[?]
miles from Eastbourne. As for four centuries past, the monarch was accompanied
pike-armed members of the Bodyguard of the Yeomen of the Guard ('Beefeaters[?]
The State Coach dates from the eighteenth century

Her Majesty Queen Elizabeth II, crowned and in a robe of white fur, rides to the op[?]
ing of a modern Parliament. On this occasion, Her Majesty used a semi-state clo[?]
carriage and was accompanied by a Sovereign's Escort of the Royal Life Guards.
the background is the House of Lords

No longer royal—though his high office descends from that of a ruler of independent London before Britain was a kingdom—the Lord Mayor of London traditionally keeps up almost royal state. Every year the new Lord Mayor travels in procession from his 'palace' of the Mansion House to pay his respects to the Sovereign. Accompanied by an escort of pikemen supplied by the Honourable Artillery Company, 'My Lord Mayor' travels in this splendid eighteenth-century coach

Armand Fallières, the great families left their London palaces and joined with their king, Edward VII, to attend the Command Performance at the Royal Opera House, Covent Garden.

The motor-car had arrived; indeed, King Edward had been amongst the first and most enthusiastic of the motor-car's admirers. But it was still new and not yet sufficiently established, despite royal patronage, to seem a fitting vehicle for so important an occasion as this. So out came the coaches, driven by the head coachmen in livery, with cockaded tricorne or tall hats on their grey-powdered wigs, with the liveried footmen strap-hanging at the rear, ready to jump off and let down the steps as soon as the coaches drew up at their destination.

The power of instant decision was one of the characteristics which most impressed those who met Holmes. Here, in John Charlton's sketch of an episode in Holmes's life not recorded in Watson's writings, we see how little Holmes cared for mere *appearances* when there was 'mischief afoot'. Finding himself in a district where cabs or hansoms were not to be had, Holmes called to a passing costermonger: 'A sovereign for the use of your barrow—it's a matter of life and death!' So here is Holmes, in a coster's 'shay', checking the 'moke' as an untypically clean-shaven policeman holds up the traffic at a typically muddy London crossing. Little does the stocking-capped brewer's drayman realise, as he addresses coarse and unwelcome badinage to the bewigged

The diamonds, the furs, the sense of being rulers . . . this was what one saw; and looked back upon with amaze, to find that it has all vanished. But in 1908 this noble blaze of aristocracy seemed to belong to a society which was immortal, as one looked at it on that calm May night over sixty years ago.

Though Holmes had retired to a house at Cuckmere Haven, five miles from Eastbourne, on the southern slopes of the Sussex Downs, he was in London on that memorable night. For, as an officer of the Legion of Honour, and one, moreover, who had rendered such signal services to the French Republic—the tracking and arrest of Huret, the Boulevard Assassin (who intended to murder the then French President) in 1895; his successful experiments at Montpellier University in the previous year; and, three years earlier than that, 'A Matter of Supreme Importance to the French Government'—Holmes's invitation from the French Embassy in London to attend the reception given by the French President may be taken for granted. And he would have received a

The Bank of England—'The Old Lady of Threadneedle Street'—in the days when London was the unchallenged commercial and financial centre of the world and the Bank, not then nationalised, financed most of the top-secret undercover operations for which Holmes was extensively employed; such affairs, for instance, as 'The Commission for the Sultan of Turkey.'

command from King Edward VII, whom he had served well without liking him, to attend the grand banquet at Buckingham Palace to celebrate the Entente Cordiale. The Lord Mayor would not have wished to be deficient in the courtesies displayed by King and President, and would doubtless have welcomed the opportunity to pay tribute to Britain's, nay, the world's most famous consulting detective by inviting him to the luncheon at the Guildhall on 30 May 1908 at which President Fallières was presented with the Freedom of the City of London, in the presence of over one thousand guests drawn from among the cream of British and French society.

The surroundings in which Holmes once again found himself at that Buckingham Palace dinner must have revived old memories, for it was not always to Windsor that the Queen summoned Holmes, to discuss with him some new scandal threatening the prestige and stability of the monarchy—the Prince of Wales's gambling and woman-chasing, the ghastly revelation of Lord Arthur Somerset's unnatural vice (for Lord Arthur, of the Blues, had been the Prince's Superintendent of the Stables and Extra Equerry when he bolted for France), the threat of the Prince's erstwhile boon-companion, Lord Charles Beresford, who, quarrelling with his royal friend over their joint passion for Lady Brooke (later Countess of Warwick), threatened to call in the Press and Telegraph associations and make public the details of a truly royal scandal.

The Buckingham Palace of George IV's redesigning had not been swept away when Victoria and Albert succeeded King William IV ('Silly Billy'). It still housed the interior decorations that George IV had transferred from Carlton House when the latter was pulled down in 1828 to make way for the new opening from Pall Mall into St James's Park. Indeed, except for the necessarily highly Victorian contemporary furnishings, Buckingham Palace, even at the height of Victorian taste, was always far more late Georgian than Victorian—as it is to-day far more late Georgian than neo-Elizabethan.

On his many visits to Buckingham Palace, most of the rooms, large and small, would have become familiar to Holmes: the smaller rooms when consulting privately with the Queen and, after he had become King, her eldest son. Holmes would have come to know the magnificent Marble (or Pillar) Room on the ground floor, as

BUCKINGHAM PALACE AS HOLMES KNEW IT

(*Left*) The Picture Gallery, about 1887, when Holmes's work on behalf of various European royalties had earned him well-merited acceptance at Queen Victoria's Court

ght) The famous Marble
ircase up which guests at a
rawing Room ' ascended to
ir reception by Her Majesty
Queen. A drawing made
ut the time of the Golden
ilee, 1887. (*Below*) The
lar Room in which Holmes
st often have sat awaiting
royal summons to enter
Queen's private apartments

well as the Throne Room, in which Queen or Prince received the Sovereign's subjects, and the Ball Room, to which allusion has already been made.

The two latter rooms, forming part of the State Apartments, are situated on the first (American second) storey, and are approached by what, as was written in 1889, 'the finest architectural effect in the palace, the grand staircase of white marble'. Fortunately, that description still applies in every particular to-day, save that the Victorian furnishings—and more importantly the Victorian colour scheme—have been replaced with an interior decoration in modern and, in my opinion, far better, taste.

To-day, only two of the royal palaces are used as homes: Buckingham Palace and Kensington Palace, residence of HRH Princess Margaret Countess of Snowdon, who shares the Palace with the London Museum, transferred here a few years ago when Lancaster House, St James's, was allocated by the government to the reception of envoys from the independent countries of 'the Commonwealth'.

Kensington Palace, originally Nottingham House, was built as the London residence of Heneage Finch, Earl of Nottingham, Lord Chancellor of England, who, suffering from asthma, found his health better in the then distant village of Kensington than it had been in London. In 1690, Finch's son, the second earl, sold the house to William III for £18,000, and in 1691 it was reconstructed by the great Sir Christopher Wren, architect of St Paul's Cathedral and Hampton Court (the modern part), and of over thirty churches in the City of London, many of which are still standing. In addition to numerous other buildings, civic and religious—the Guildhall, at Rochester, is his work—he designed for America. There is a (restored) original building of his design in Williamsburg, Virginia.

The tendency to reduce the number of royal palaces actually used as residences began as early as 1861 when Queen Victoria decided to move the holding of levées* and drawing-room receptions from St James's Palace to Buckingham Palace; however, there are still some 'grace and favour' apartments in St James's Palace, in which live certain persons of reduced means who have rendered exceptional service to the royal family.

---

*The levée returned to St James's Palace after the death of the Prince Consort, the Prince of Wales receiving gentlemen on behalf of his mother.

Both Clarence House, St James's, built for the Duke of Clarence, afterwards King William IV, and later renovated for the Duke of Edinburgh, son of Queen Victoria, on his marriage to the Grand Duchess Marie of Russia, and Marlborough House, next-door to St James's Palace, built by Wren in 1710 for the first Duke of Marlborough (it became Crown property in 1817), have been used as royal residences within very recent times. For many years after her husband's death in 1936 Marlborough House was the residence of Queen Mary, wife of King George V, and it was in Clarence House that Princess Margaret, before her marriage, lived with her mother, Queen Elizabeth the Queen Mother, who still lives there.

The Houses of Parliament, rebuilt by Sir Charles Barry between 1840 and 1859 at a cost of about £3,000,000, replace the old Houses, almost completely destroyed in the fire of 1834, caused by the careless burning of wooden 'tally sticks', a primitive method of computation and record on which, up to that time, the national accounts of the great British Empire had been kept. Adjoining the rebuilt Houses, of which the 350-ft Victoria Tower (known to all Londoners as 'Big Ben') is the most eye-catching feature, is the eleventh century Westminster Hall, in which General de Gaulle, after the French nation had voted him their President, addressed both Chambers of Parliament, Commons and Peers: an historic occasion that those who witnessed it will never forget.

Enlarged by Richard II in 1398, and vandalistically shortened by Barry so as to accommodate his plans for his fake-Gothic, Westminster Hall, 290ft long and 92ft high, is still one of the longest halls in the world having a roof unsupported by columns.

I have introduced the Houses of Parliament here because, officially, this complex of old and new buildings (including Roman foundations, a Norman crypt and Jewel House, medieval rooms, seventeenfh and eighteenth century erections of one use and another) is 'the Palace of Westminster' and by far the oldest of all London's royal palaces, even though it is centuries since any English monarch lived there.

Not long after the rebuilding, there was serious agitation to transfer Parliament in its entirety to Hampton Court Palace, fifteen miles up-river from Westminster. The reason for this agitation was the appalling stench which often made it necessary to suspend Parliamentary business, and caused the half-asphyxiated members to rush out on the terrace overlooking the Thames to breathe what seemed to them (by comparison) fresh air from the filthy river.

What had happened was this: the Victorian jerry-builders had covered an open sewer, which ran right through the new buildings, with only a single skin of relatively thin stone slab; it was through this very permeable skin that the smells of the sewer were arising. Remedial work soon put an end to the nuisance and Parliament has met, for what that is worth, in Barry's buildings ever since, save for a time during the second World War when, because of the demolition, by bombing, of the debating chamber of the House of Commons (10 May 1941), the members had to make do with temporary accommodation. However, at a cost of £1,000,000, a much more convenient chamber was provided, which was opened by King George VI on 26 October 1950. Sir Giles Gilbert Scott, grandson of the architect of St Pancras Station and the Albert Memorial—with his son, Adrian—were the architects.

There is another royal palace, the Tower of London, to be considered, but I shall write of that in a later chapter when we consider Holmes's activities in the eastern part of the City, especially in those dark places which once lay on both sides of The Pool of London.

The other London palaces, so plentiful and so well known to Holmes in the days before the first World War, were those of the great families, all of whom maintained at least one large London mansion and one very much larger 'seat' in the country. There were few really great families which did not have at least half-a-dozen.

I take *Debrett's Peerage, Baronetage and Knightage* for 1900 out of the bookshelf and turn up at random the head of the House of Grosvenor, His Grace the Duke of Westminster, KG, PC, born 18 October 1825. I quote: '*Seats*: Eaton Hall, Chester; Halkin, Flintshire. *Town Residence*: 38 Upper Grosvenor Street, W.'—an address which modestly hides the identity of the ultra-luxurious Grosvenor House, demolished in 1927, on whose site was erected, shortly afterwards, one of London's biggest hotels. The old Grosvenor House, built in 1842 to the designs of the Westminsters' principal private architect, Cundy, was of unprecedented splendour, even for a London nobleman's house. It contained one of the finest collections of Old Masters in the world, many of which are now in the United States.

Not one of these noblemen's palaces is still in private tenancy, and the majority have been sold by their tax-oppressed owners, and blocks of flats or hotels have arisen on their sites. But some of the original buildings remain, and from them we may obtain some idea of the lavish way of life enjoyed in these London mansions before two World Wars pauperised Britain and deprived it of 'Society' in any recognisable former meaning of the word.

Crewe House, Curzon Street, once the town house of the Marquess of Crewe, is one. Erected in 1735, it was purchased by the first Earl (later Marquess) of Crewe in 1899 for £90,000, and was the scene of memorable dinners for which the famous Mrs Rosa Lewis was called in as *cordon bleu chef-de-cuisine*. Bought in 1937 by Thomas Tilling & Co, then big public transport owners, the house remains in possession of the firm, which, though using it as offices, has carefully maintained its splendid outward appearance.

Opposite, at the corner of Curzon Street and Trebeck Street, is Sunderland House, one of the last great private houses to be built in London. Of a dark, gloomy, 'cyclopean' style of architecture, it was a wedding present from his American mother to the 9th Duke of Manchester. It, too, has been used as exhibition hall and offices for more than thirty years.

Londonderry House, at the corner of Hertford Street and Park Lane, across the road from the new London Hilton Hotel, was built in 1850. It was the town residence of the Marquesses of Londonderry, and has recently been replaced by an hotel.

In nearby South Audley Street was Chesterfield House, erected in 1750 for Philip Dormer, 4th Earl of Chesterfield. Before its demolition in 1934 it was the residence of the late Princess Mary, Princess Royal, and her husband, the Earl of Harewood. It was a stone-built mansion which had been constructed of material from the unfinished palace, called 'Canons', built by the Duke of Chandos at Edgware, in Middlesex.

But nothing, not even the royal palaces, could rival in splendour the mansion erected by Vulliamy in 1851 for the Holford family, who had not even a title to excuse all this magnificence. Built in the Italian style, Dorchester House, Park Lane, was, in Clunn's words, 'a magnificent mansion probably second to none in the metropolis'.

It had a marble staircase which, even in 1851, had cost £30,000; when the house was pulled down in 1929, this marble staircase was knocked down to Mrs Rosa Lewis, owner of the famous Cavendish Hotel in Jermyn Street, for less than £100!

Occupied at various times by such notables as the Shah of Persia, its last most distinguished tenant was Whitelaw Reid, the American Ambassador, but even he found it too costly to run, and the house, after having been occupied for only seventy-eight years, was pulled down and the present Dorchester Hotel erected on its site.

However, a number of these former palaces of the nobility and landed gentry still exist, unaltered outwardly since the day when they formed commonplaces of Sherlock Holme's far, far richer London.

Here is a representative selection of the survivors: —

House	Former owner/family
Wimborne House, Arlington Street (Next door to Ritz Hotel)	Lord Wimborne
Lancaster House, St James's	Duke of Sutherland
Apsley House (Partly a museum: the Duke of Wellington now having apartments on the upper floors)	Duke of Wellington
Spencer House, St James's Place	Earl Spencer
Chatham House, St James's Square	William Pitt; Earl of Derby; Mr Gladstone (three Prime Ministers)
Hertford House, Manchester Square (Now houses the Wallace Collection)	Duke of Manchester; Sir Richard Wallace
Harrington House, Craig's Court, Whitehall (First turning on left from Trafalgar Square)	Earls of Harrington
Lansdowne House, Berkeley Square	Marquess of Bute (Minister to George III)

44 Berkeley Square (Now the Clermont Club)	Earls of Powis
Cambridge House, Piccadilly (Now the Naval & Military Club)	Duke of Cambridge; Lord Palmerston
Stanhope House, Stanhope Gate (Now offices)	Robert Hudson, the 'Soap King'
French Embassy, Albert Gate	George Hudson, the 'Railway King'
97 Park Lane (Now offices)	Lord Beaconsfield
28 Curzon Street (Now the White Elephant Club)	Lord Beaconsfield
Lindsey House (Now six houses, including the Royal Historical Society)	Count Zinzendorff (Imperial Chancellor, 18th Century)
Tredegar House, Farm Street (The last private mansion to be built in London, with the exception of Miss Barbara Hutton's Winfield House, Regent's Park)	Viscounts Tredegar
Burlington House (Now the Royal Academy)	Earls of Burlington

Gwydyr House (1772), Whitehall
(RAF Recruitment Centre)

. . . and, of course, most of the surviving houses in Regent's Park, Park Crescent, Portland Place, Queen Anne's Gate (houses built early in the eighteenth century by William Paterson, founder of the Bank of England), Harley Street, Wimpole Street, Chesterfield Gardens (Curzon Street), Kensington Palace Gardens, Connaught Place and such parts of Hyde Park and Lancaster Gate as are still standing, together with the surviving houses of Palace Gate and Hyde Park Gate, in which Sir Winston Churchill died.

The visitor to London should not miss No 1 Palace Gate, a mansion built and lived in by the President of the Royal Academy, Sir John Everett Millais, Baronet, who, once he had 'arrived', painted only three portraits a year, at a fixed fee of five thousand guineas the portrait. No matter what was offered him to paint more, he stuck rigidly to his rule to accept only three commissions a year.

His house is worth studying, not because of any outstanding architectural merit—it has little—but because it demonstrates how a successful painter, of no particular birth and of provincial origin (like his successful contemporary and friend, Lily Langtry, he came from Jersey), could, in late Victorian times, range himself in social prestige no less than in wealth with the genuinely upper-crust of English Society.

Watson, in his discretion, concealed the true identity of people and places known to Holmes under what appear to us to be the most randomly selected pseudonyms.

Take the peers who enter into the Canon:—

The Duke of Holdernesse, the Duke of Greyminster,* the Duke of Belminster, the Earl of Backwater, the Earl of Dovercourt, the Prince of Colonna, Lord Balmoral, Lord Bellinger, Lord Cantlemere, Lord Harringby, Lord Holdhurst, Lord Leverstoke, Lord Mount-James.

And take the peeresses, 'courtesy titles', baronets and knights:—

Lady Eva Blackwell, Lady Mary Brackenstall, Sir George Burnwell, Countess d'Albert, Sir James Damery, Lady Beatrice Falder, Sir George Ffolliot, Sir John Hardy, Sir Edward Holly, the Honourable Miss Miles, the Countess of Morcar, Sir John Morland, Sir Robert Norberton, Lord Robert St Simon, Sir Cathcart Soames, Sir Leslie Oakshott, Sir Jabez Gilchrist, the Honourable Philip Green, Lady Spender, Count Negretto Silvius, Lady Alice Whittington, Baron Adalbert Gruner, Lady Maynooth, and the rest.

Even after all these years, it would be indiscreet to lift the veil on Watson's discretion, yet the names are so very nearly similar to the correct ones.

But no matter. Let us leave the names as Watson left them, and merely remark here that if Holmes called only once on all these titled persons, he would have known the inside of nearly forty of London's better houses. And this is not to take account of all those other houses in which, though untitled, persons of what used to be called 'very comfortable means' lived exceedingly comfortably. Leaving aside the sixteen Service officers above the military rank

*But 'Holdernesse' and 'Greyminster' may be the same. See page 199.

of captain, and the several civilian professional men of standing, with all of whom Holmes had business relations—and in those days even the meanest and most poverty-stricken had at least one servant —there were other well-furnished establishments into which he would have entered.

For instance, though Holmes did not enter the house of 'the worst man in London', Charles Augustus Milverton, as a guest, it was into no humble suburban villa that he stepped when he called on Milverton at Appledore Towers, Hampstead. And though he entered Briony Lodge, Serpentine Avenue, St John's Wood, only by means of a trick and to recover a letter whose existence was troubling the peace of the 'reformed' King of Bohemia, yet Holmes must have spared a moment or two whilst there to be impressed by the luxury to be found in the home of a woman who was not only rich through her singing at the world's leading opera houses, but richer through having been the mistress of a king.

But for every grand house that Holmes entered, openly or furtively, in the course of his professional duties (with or without Watson), far more must have been open to him in his capacity of a personable and successful young man—he was still only thirty-three when he prevented 'a scandal in Bohemia'—whose advance in his self-chosen profession included, as all London knew, the prestige gained from having been of service to several royal families.

The year 1887, in which Holmes was able to be of service to the King of Bohemia, was the year of Queen Victoria's Golden Jubilee; a year in which a six-weeks' spell of completely rainless summer, though worrying to the farmers, seemed to the rest of the population to be something of a divine benediction on the Queen and her people. Yet, despite the almost hysterical chauvinism of that year: the flag-waving, the naval and military reviews, the receptions and garden parties and mayoral banquets and the 'treats' to elderly paupers and hardly more wealthy board-school children, there was unrest in the air. That unrest actually erupted into bitter violence in November 1887, when the Life Guards were called out to sabre a rioting mob of unemployed in Trafalgar Square: a mob which did a lot of damage to 'respectable' property before it was subdued and sent back along the wet, cold, dreary road which leads from Trafalgar Square to the Mile End Road, Bethnal Green, Poplar and Stepney.

The headquarters of the Metropolitan Police in Great Scotland Yard, Charing Cross. It was here, on 30 May 1884, at 9.20 pm, that a bomb exploded, wrecking the police department and severely damaging the 'snug' of the nearby 'Clarence' public-house, seen on the right of the arch. The rebuilt 'Clarence' is still in service

Rioting in the Queen's Golden Jubilee Year! Who would ever have conceived that international revolutionary socialism, brought over from Austria, Germany, France, Italy and Russia by the proscribed philosophers of the First International, would have made the English working-class man so forgetful of his duties to those whom God had placed over him? But he did forget, and the inept Commissioner of Police for the Metropolitan Area, General Sir Charles Warren, GCMG, who was to fail to find (or to expose) 'Jack the Ripper' in the following year, could provide no better solution to 'illegal demonstrations' than to ask the Home Secretary to authorise the use of troops. No wonder that (in 'The Five Orange Pips') Holmes refers to 'the imbecility' of the police!

But the rigid divisions of caste were already softening and crumbling, apart from any pressure by professional revolutionaries or unemployed workers. It is said that London Society was 'shocked' when Lily Langtry entertained a party of guests in the dining-room of the then newly-opened Grand Hotel (opened June 1880, it was 'built in the Italian style') but dining-out in London's new and elegant hotels soon became a fad of the rich. And if, for the first time in history, they abandoned their homes for restaurants, they brought more of the world back into their homes than would have been thought possible only a decade before.

The anonymous author of *The Glass of Fashion: A Universal Handbook of Social Etiquette and Home Culture for Ladies and Gentlemen*, published in 1881, has detected and realistically commented upon a fundamental change which has overtaken society:

> Presentations at Court are valued because they place the persons so favoured within the charmed circle of fashionable Society, and confer upon them a definite social position. They are, therefore, very properly fenced round with certain restrictions, though these are not so rigid as they were in the days of the Georges. Formerly, only persons of undisputed rank and breeding claimed access to the royal presence; but this privilege is now extended to the clergy, military and naval officers, physicians and barristers, and their wives and daughters, as well as to the families of merchants, bankers, members of the Stock Exchange, and manufacturers of the higher class. Artists and litterateurs of repute are also admitted, but [my italics] *not necessarily or usually any member of their families.*

It was the inclusion of 'litterateurs of repute', and the usual exclusion of their families which caused Charles Dickens to refuse permission for his daughter to act in a charity performance at Windsor Castle unless the Queen 'received' Miss Dickens—a piece of blackmail with which we may sympathise but which is said to have cost Dickens his expected knighthood.

If such rag-tag-and-bobtail as 'physicians and barristers . . . as well as merchants, bankers, members of the Stock Exchange, and manufacturers of the higher class' were now admitted to Court, then we may hardly doubt that Holmes, for all his unique and unprecedented profession, would have attended one or more of the Prince of Wales's levées (for gentlemen only of course) at St James's Palace, and—Holmes being Holmes—he would probably have 'wangled' a presentation for his friend, Watson, who, as a half-pay officer, could have made his reverence to his Sovereign's Heir in regulation uniform. Holmes, of course, would have worn civilian court dress.

> . . . if we are civilians, without any rank, inherited or acquired, we attire ourselves in court dress, either of cloth or velvet. When the suit is of cloth, it consists of claret-coloured trousers, with a narrow gold stripe down the side; dress coat, single breasted, with broad collar, cuffs and pocket flaps; white waistcoat and white tie, cocked hat and sword. When the dress is of velvet, the coat is emblazoned with bright steel buttons, and instead of trousers, knee-breeches, with silk stockings, shoes and buckles, are worn. The colour for velvet is black. Gentlemen attending levées wear gloves, but usually remove the right-hand glove before entering the Throne Room, in case the Prince of Wales* should be pleased to shake hands with them—an honour reserved, however, for those with whom he is personally acquainted.

Certainly by the time Holmes's application to be presented at Court was made and granted, the Prince would have become personally acquainted with him, and though it has been remarked that Holmes did not like the Prince, yet that mark of royal favour, the hand-shake, would hardly have been denied to the man who had done so much to avert scandal from the royal family.

---

*At the four levées each year, the Prince of Wales represented the Queen.

And even though, disapproving of the 'playboy' attitude of the Prince, he disliked his future king, Holmes had love as well as loyalty for his Queen. Why, otherwise, would he have picked out his Gracious Sovereign's initials in bullet-pocks on the wall of 221B, as lesser men carve their ladylove's initials on a tree-trunk?

CHAPTER 5

Sherlock Goes East

One of the most dramatic, though least successful, episodes in the long saga of Holmes's professional career is that down-river chase of Jonathan Small in the evening of 20 September 1888.

How the deceptively unemotional prose of Watson's narrative style brings not only the drama but the physical surrounding of that drama so vividly to our eyes that it is hard to believe it all happened nearly a century ago.

Chasing Jonathan Small, who was making for his vessel, the *Esmeralda*, 'at Gravesend, outward bound for the Brazils', Holmes, learning that Small has taken off in a fast steam-launch, the *Aurora*, commandeers a police boat to follow Small down-river.

It was a little past seven before we reached Westminster Wharf, and found our launch awaiting us. Holmes eyed it critically.

'Is their anything to mark it as a police boat?'

'Yes; the green lamp at the side'.

'Then take it off'.

The small change was made, we stepped on board, and the ropes were cast off. Jones, Holmes, and I sat in the stern. There was one man at the rudder, one to tend the engines, and two burly police inspectors, forward.

'Where to?' asked Jones.

'To the Tower. Tell them to stop opposite Jacobson's Yard.'

Our craft was evidently a fast one. We shot past the long lines of loaded barges as though they were stationary.

110

Headquarters of the Thames Police, High Street, Wapping, in 1891. Holmes, in usual inverness (but wearing a bowler) is stepping into a police launch, whilst Watson, formal as ever in dark overcoat, bowler and high collar, follows down the slippery steps. Some of these old Thames-side houses are left: notably the ' Prospect of Whitby ' and 'Angel' taverns, the first at Wapping, the second at Shadwell

An inspector and two constables of the Thames Police take off
in a two-paired launch, whilst another constable gives their boat
a helpful shove. Though the year is 1891, the men still wear the
black glazed 'boater' adopted when the police were organised as
the private 'Preventative Service' in 1792

One of the three steam launches leaving the station of the Thames
Police at London Bridge. It was in a police launch of this type that
Holmes and Watson chased Jonathan Small and the murderous
Andaman Islander in *The Sign of Four*

Blackfriars Bridge, through one of whose arches Holmes's police launch shot, as he gave chase to Jonathan Small

St Paul's Cathedral, as Holmes saw it from the river in his pursuit of Small

Though much rebuilding has taken place since the bombing of World War II, the riverside scene is curiously unchanged from its late Victorian aspect, as this modern view shows

Holmes smiled with satisfaction as we overhauled a river steamer and left her behind us.

'We ought to be able to catch anything on the river,' he said.

'Well, hardly that. But there are not many launches to beat us.'

'We shall have to catch the *Aurora,* and she has a name for being a clipper. I will tell you how the land lies, Watson . . .'

And catch the *Aurora* they do, though only after one of the most exciting river chases in literature. And only, alas, after the Great Agra Treasure (loot worth 'half a million of money') had gone overboard, perhaps to be found one day when they are dredging

London Bridge, opened in 1832; its stone casing is now in California and another wider London Bridge has taken its place. Here it is as Holmes saw it on his dash down the river. Fishmonger's Hall, splendid home of the Fishmongers' Company, still stands on the left of the bridge, as does the church of St Magnus the Martyr on the right

'As we passed the City the last rays of the sun were gilding the cross upon the summit of St. Paul's. It was twilight before we reached the Tower.'—so Watson in his narrative of *The Sign of Four* described the scene. Here is the Tower of London by a twilight of September 1888

the Thames, where Barking Level lies upon one side and 'the melancholy Plumstead Marshes upon the other'.

Much which seems familiar in this narrative of close on a century ago—'As we passed the City the last rays of the sun were gilding the cross upon the summit of St Paul's. It was twilight before we reached the Tower.'—tends to obscure the fact that it is along this same river that London, in the years since Holmes's chase of the *Aurora,* but more importantly since the end of World War II, has undergone some of its most radical changes, with even more radical changes projected or actually taking place.

St Paul's is still with us, still falling down, still in need of a large sum of money (it is £3,000,000 this time) to 'preserve the fabric', but still, one feels, good to last against anything but bombing for centuries to come. The Tower is still with us, and cleaner now than in Holmes's day, for the steam brush has begun to clean up London, though not to the same extent that it has cleaned up Paris.

Still, it is a cleaner if not more beautiful London that we have

The Tower floodlit—a modern photograph. London's most famous fortress and repository of Britain's Crown Jewels, the Tower has grown over the centuries from a Roman fort, the Norman kings rebuilding it entirely in the eleventh and twelfth centuries

today; the people are not so clean, for they seem to have been encouraged by successive governments to lose most of their self-respect, and the quality of being 'house-proud' is far rarer than it was. But, at least, smoke-abatement regulations have combined with the replacement of the steam locomotive by diesel trains to purify London's air, and so keep the city's buildings less smoke-grimed than they were in Holmes's day.

But if, in reading of Holmes's adventures of some ninety to fifty years ago, we are given a superficial impression of identity with our own world, there are random remarks which tell us how greatly all has changed. For instance: ' "That is Jacobson's Yard", said Holmes, pointing to a bristle of masts and rigging on the Surrey side.'

Overlooking the Watsonian error—he says 'Surrey' here, when he means 'Kent'—we realise that we are in another world than theirs: a world in which, though steamships with electric light were crossing the Atlantic in under five days, the sailing-ship was still the commoner; not until the next century was steam to over-take sail. And another point: London was then not only one of the world's greatest ports, if not the greatest, but was in process of being expanded to rival any other that might be built anywhere in the world in the near or distant future.

The conversion of the eastern suburban hamlets and villages into docks was begun as a result of the congestion caused by ships in mid-river awaiting their turn to discharge at the 'legal quays' of the Thames, monopolistic preserves of the City of London, existing under legislation passed in Elizabeth I's day.

There had been docks at Greenwich and Woolwich since before Henry VIII's day, but 'docks', in the modern sense of the word did not exist in London proper until the imperative necessities of the French war (usually called the Napoleonic war) made the con-version of London into a properly equipped port a matter of vital urgency. Until that date, ships, no matter how important or needed their cargoes, had to anchor in mid-river, awaiting their turn to off-load at one of the 'legal quays'. Too often, off-loading had to be done in mid-stream by lighter, an operation which, as has been described by Marryat and Dickens and other writers, generated an industry of thieving, every aspect of which had its own highly specialised practitioners.

It was on one of the boats of the Thames Police Force that

The more sinister side of the Tower: the Place of Execution. Here soldiers of the last century practise for the firing-squad, to which Holmes's Secret Service activities brought several victims

Dickens traversed the grey length of the river from Battersea to Wapping—'where the old Thames Police office is now a station-house'—and learnt the names of the categories into which the river-thieves were divided.

There were the Tier-rangers, who 'ranged' along the tiers of shipping, and whose peculiar skill it was to enter the cabins of ships' officers whilst the occupants were asleep, and to rob both sleepers and cabins. There were the Lumpers—larcenist-dockers, the specially large pockets of whose loose canvas coats were filled with the goods they had abstracted in the course of their unloading ships' cargoes. Any goods too large to go ashore in the Lumpers' pockets were landed by the Truckers; while the Dredger-men's art was to throw goods into the river for subsequent dredging-up and sale.

Then there were the Watermen, whose jobs included anything from ferrying a traveller across the Thames to finding a 'stiff 'un' floating on the tide; for even the bodies of pauper suicides were clothed, and clothes of any sort, in those days, would fetch something. It is as he is on the look-out for waterlogged corpses that we meet Gaffer Hexham, in *Our Mutual Friend*; but the best description of a waterman's life—watermen were apprenticed and, 'out of their articles', licensed—is to be found in Marryat's *Jacob Faithful*.

If such plundering of ships' cargoes was taking place fifty and sixty years after a start had been made on providing London with docks, one may imagine on what a wholesale scale was the plunder in the years before 1805, when, on 30 January (Feast of St Charles, King and Martyr), London Docks were opened. They covered an area of one hundred acres, and had cost £4,000,000—exactly the sum that the British Government had wasted by giving it to the United States Government to purchase Louisiana from Napoleon I (to whom it did not belong).

During the century, other, and greater, docks joined London Docks in making London 'the greatest port in the world'. Next came St Katherine Docks, extending from Tower Hill, by the Tower of London on the west, to Nightingale Lane on the east, and Upper East Smithfield on the north. Ours is not the only generation which can undertake gigantic plans and carry them through with rapidity. A whole parish, including the ancient Royal Hospital of St Katherine (of which portions still remain), was demolished, and no fewer than 11,300 inhabitants rehoused in new property, quite a lot of which still survives in the streets which lie between Whitechapel and the Thames.

The first stone of St Katherine Docks was laid with appropriate ceremony on 3 May 1827, and the docks were officially declared open on 25 October 1828. It had taken slightly less than eighteen months to build them, with 'earth-moving equipment' no more sophisticated than shovels, baskets and horses-and-carts. The job necessitated the demolition of 1,250 houses and the old hospital, the clearing and excavation of the site (including the building of extensive coffer-dams), the quarrying, shaping, dressing and transportation of vast quantities of granite, and the making and providing of the thousand-and-one accessories without which no dock may function. And all in less than eighteen months.

St Katherine Docks took, as they say, 'a right bashing' in the Blitz, notably during the Battle of Britain at the end of 1940. Almost every one of the docks' warehouses backing on East Smithfield were damaged or destroyed, and those which were razed to the ground have not been, and will not be, rebuilt. In time, all that remains of St Katherine's—now no more than accommodation for dredgers and small craft—will have vanished, its place taken by the proposed 'tree-lined riverside promenade, with parks, restaurants, cafés and concert-halls extending from Tower Hill Gardens to King Edward VII Park. The present riverside wall will then disappear'. This 'developers' ' Sabbath has already begun with the emptying and demolition of those miles of riverside warehouses whose grim functional ugliness so fascinated the great French artist, Gustave Doré. In the reign of Elizabeth I, St Katherine's was the district of the great London breweries, which supplied beer to the English armies fighting in the Netherlands.

But when Holmes, Watson and Athelney Jones, of Scotland Yard, sped down-river at the heels of Jonathan Small and his murderous Andaman Islander chum, London, as a port, was still in active development with its greatest days yet to come.

> We had shot through the Pool, past the West India Docks, down the long Deptford Reach, and up again, after rounding the Isle of Dogs . . . At Greenwich we were about three hundred paces behind them. At Blackwall we could not have been more than two hundred and fifty. I have coursed many creatures in many countries during my chequered career, but never did sport give me such a wild thrill as this mad, flying man-hunt down the Thames. Steadily we drew in upon them, yard by yard . . .

So, yard by yard, the distance was decreased between them— 'in the silence of the night we could hear the panting and clanking of their machinery', even though 'our boilers were strained to their utmost, and the frail shell vibrated and creaked with the fierce energy which was driving us along'.

Of course, though this point has not been raised before, the ability of Holmes and his party to hear the 'panting and clanking' of the pursued vessel, even though the police-boat 'vibrated and creaked with the fierce energy' which was driving it along, may suggest that the police-boat was jet-propelled—a type of propulsion not uncommon in the late 1880s.

A 'jet-propeller-engine', says Capt H. Paasch, in his best-selling *Illustrated Marine Encyclopedia,** is 'one constructed to drive a vessel by the reaction of the water, caused by jets of water or steam being forced from the interior of the vessel through tubular outlets or apertures . . . '.

---

*Antwerp, 1890: published by the author, 27 rue d'Amsterdam.

But by whatever means Holmes and the others shot down-river, it was obviously one of those occasions when the importance and all-engrossing excitement of the chase prevented even such diversions as Holmes's glancing at his stop-watch in order to calculate the speed at which they were chasing the *Aurora*.

They saw what was flashing by on both sides of the river, but they saw these things with unseeing eyes; all their attentions caught by the boat ahead, in which 'I could see old Smith, stripped to the waist, . . . against the red glare of the furnace . . . and shovelling coals for dear life'. They passed buildings which are still with us, and buildings which vanished decades ago. Of what they saw with unseeing eyes that September evening in 1888, these are still with us: Big Ben and the Houses of Parliament, the Thames Embankment, as far as Blackfriars, the Avenue (renamed the Playhouse) Theatre and the tall hotels in Northumberland Avenue; Charing Cross railway bridge and station, the Duke of Buckingham's watergate under the Adelphi, Adam houses in the Adelphi, Somerset House, the then new 'Tudor' houses in Surrey Street, Arundel Street and Norfolk Street, with the spires of St Clement Danes and the new Royal Courts of Justice (completed 1882, to the designs of G. E. Street, RA) beyond. The riverside churches: St Mary Somerset, by Puddle Dock, St Laurence Pountney, St Magnus the Martyr (long ago the temple of Kybebe Magna Mater—'Kybebe, the Great Mother'), helping Fishmongers' Hall (home of one of the City's richest livery companies; its income, as far back as 1890, was over £20,000 a year) to flank London Bridge.

They passed still-standing Billingsgate Fish Market, the 1814-17 Laing-Smirke Custom House, with the spires of all the Wren churches around and behind the river-front buildings: St Margaret Pattens, St Mary-at-Hill, St Olave Hart Street, St Andrew Undershaft, St Edmund King and Martyr, St Dunstan-in-the-East, St Botolph Aldgate. They shot past the open water outside the Tower, over the Thames Subway (opened in 1869: the world's first tunnel to be built with the Greathead shield), with no Tower Bridge above (that would not come until 1894) and so on down a river whose ancient, weather-boarded backs had been reflected in the muddy waters these past three centuries and more. Nearly all have gone; though one or two taverns—the much-frequented 'Prospect of Whitby' and 'The Town of Ramsgate', at Wapping Old Stairs, which, some say, was the pub on which Dickens based his famous 'The Six Jolly Fellowship Porters', in *Our Mutual Friend*—remain to show us what the river-side around Shadwell and Wapping must have looked like when Holmes and Watson rushed downstream in 1888.

As we pause on the very edge of the riverside's extensive rebuild-ing, there is still much to remind us of the past. St Anne Limehouse still raises its white stone spire, and the two oldest of London's 'new' docks—the West India (begun 1800) and the East India (begun 1806)—still survive, together with later docks: Millwall, Surrey Commercial, Victoria and Royal Albert. Those docks were all which had been constructed by 1888.

Some fifty-two years later, one-third of London's warehouse space was to be blitzed, between September 1940 and May 1941. Yet, by the middle of 1945, when the war ended, London had almost recovered as a port, no less than 106 million tons of shipping having passed through London Docks at the relatively trivial cost of five hundred ships destroyed by enemy action.

As Clunn says, 'Only nine years after the day when the Thames was turned into a river of fire, the Port of London was already back in its old exalted place'.

Yet the doom of London as a port had been pronounced many years earlier, when that greatest of all tunnel-builders, Weetman Pearson, 1st Lord Cowdray, dreamed up his 'London-by-the-Sea'. This was to be a great town and port, situated about where Erith is now, and connected by an under-river road with the opposite Essex shore so that road and rail traffic could go straight from the Channel ports to the industrial centres of the Midlands and the North, without touching London.

The 'Erith Tunnel' of Pearson's dream is now a reality, and the Thames-side city-port is on its way to realisation, too. Already a vast agglomeration of houses, roughly to be described as a 'town', has risen on the Thames by Erith. It is called Thamesmead, and the 'twee' name will give those who know anything about British municipal bureaucrats a good idea of what the new 'town' must look like, without the tedious necessity of visiting it.

What else of all that Holmes and Watson might have seen on that wild, mad dash down-river remains today?

Those buildings, of course, which have been protected by a tradi-tional sentimentality stronger even than municipal ignorance and

The new Waterloo Bridge completed during World War II and replacing that built by John Rennie and opened in 1812. Originally called the Strand Bridge, and financed out of a public lottery, the first Waterloo Bridge remained a toll-bridge until 1878, the year in which Holmes began to practise in London as a private consulting detective

developers' greed: such as St Paul's Cathedral, Somerset House, the Tower, the Monument, most of Wren's churches (though the ecclesiastical hatred of City churches, finding its most viciously powerful expression in the Union of City Benefices Act, enabled the Church to destroy eleven Wren churches before 1900—more than Hitler managed to do!), and such modern but now getting-old buildings as the 'new' Law Courts in the Strand. What is new is now very evident: a new Waterloo Bridge (opened 1944), a new London Bridge, and a power-station at Bankside—where Shakespeare's Globe Theatre once stood—which pours out its oily black smoke over a city in which the 'smoke abatement' laws are enforced with considerable severity, though not, apparently, on the 'executives' of the Central Electricity Generating Board.

Some of the bridges have gone, but most of those that Holmes and Watson knew as young men are still with us: Westminster

The Tower Subway, the world's first 'tube'—that is, a tunnel driven through the earth using the Greathead Shield. Opened in 1869 to run under the Thames between Tower Hill and Pickle Herring Street, the Tower Subway was rendered obsolete as a pedestrian throughway by the opening of the Tower Bridge in 1894. Since then the Tower Subway has carried the high-pressure mains of the London Hydraulic Company, water and electric mains, and in two World Wars has served as a 'safe deposit' for national treasures

Bridge (1862), Blackfriars Bridge (1869), Tower Bridge (1894), Hungerford (railway) Bridge, 'an affront', says Clunn, rightly, 'to the appearance of the Thames Embankment, dating from 1860. Battersea Bridge (1890), the Royal Albert Suspension Bridge (1850), all

Tower Bridge, as Holmes first knew it. The twin bascules, each weighing 1,000 tons, lift to allow the passage of ships, pedestrians crossing either over the lowered bascules or by a raised footway, 142 ft. above high water and reached by staircases in the towers

date from what we may call, in a loose manner of speaking, 'Holmes's day'.

Other bridges which were familiar to him, Chelsea Suspension Bridge, Southwark Bridge and Lambeth Bridge, have since been rebuilt: respectively, in 1937, 1921 and 1927.

Yet, as Holmes and Watson would be the first to admit, despite the wholesale pulling down and rebuilding that London has undergone since, say, 1890, the *persona*—the individual *look*—of London remains, just as the face of a friend does not change just because he or she is wearing a different suit or dress, or a different style of hairdressing.

But when one boils this persistent character of a city down to its essence, one finds that this personality, this continuing idiom of character, consists in the enduring nature of but one or two highly individual, and instantly recognisable, buildings or natural features. In London, these buildings which so preserve London's recognisable character, for generation after generation, are few indeed: Westminster Abbey, the Houses of Parliament, Big Ben, the clustered spires of Whitehall Court which, since last century, have turned

The Law Courts in the Strand; they were the 'new' Law Courts when
Holmes began his practice. Opened in 1882, they replaced the congested,
inconvenient courts which used to be held in Westminster Hall

London's skyline, for a few magical moments, to that of Buda-Pesth.
Then there are St Paul's, the Nelson Column, St. Martin-in-the
Fields, the National Gallery, Burton's screen at Hyde Park Corner,
Buckingham Palace (but this was refronted only when Holmes had
turned sixty), the main railway stations ('termini', as the successors
of those whose imagination and energy made them like to call them)
—King's Cross, St Pancras, Paddington, Charing Cross (still familiar
even with the added two storeys), Marylebone (even though the Great
Central Hotel is nothing more than a shabby British Railways office
these days). Euston, or as it was called in Holmes's day, 'the Euston
Square Station', had been demolished and a bolted-together artifact
erected in its place; but, even the platforms of Cannon Street Station
are still recognisable and Waterloo Station, for all the rebuilding
of the immediate post-World War I years, has much of the old
Waterloo about it. What else? Well: the railway viaduct across the
bottom of Ludgate Hill makes Ludgate Circus familiar, for all the
rebuilding which has taken place, or will, in the near future, take
place.

London, in short, would still have a sense of familiarity to someone who returned to it after an absence of even a century. Visually, no less than spiritually, the London of Sherlock Holmes shares important similarities with the London of today.

What has gone are those links, most obvious in Holmes's day, with the past of as far back as late medieval times. Where Australia House (1913-18, but, in its 'Imperial' magnificence, one of the finest Edwardian buildings in existence) and Bush House (1920-35) now stand at the end of Kingsway (officially opened by King Edward VII and Queen Alexandra on 18 October 1905), was, in Holmes's day, a maze of streets, centred about Little Queen Street. This maze was known under the collective name of Clare Market, and included such well-known London streets as Holywell Street, Wych Street, Newcastle Street and Clare Market itself, a fragment of which, with its eighteenth-century houses, still remains. Demolition of this maze began in 1900-01, as part of the 'improvements' to the Strand already decided upon as far back as 1816. Demolition, in the case of the area lying between the Strand on the south and Southampton Row on the north, involved not merely the demolition of three theatres— the 'old' Gaiety (formerly the Strand Music Hall and not to be confused with the present Strand Theatre), the Olympic, and the Globe (there is now another Globe, in Shaftesbury Avenue)—and the famous old Coach and Horses Hotel which fronted the north side of the Strand, but also the sweeping away of many acres of buildings, many of them dating from the sixteenth and even the fifteenth century and almost none later than the seventeenth century, which had miraculously survived into the twentieth century. Other great cities —Paris, Amsterdam, Rotterdam, Berne, Geneva, Prague, Copenhagen, Warsaw, Nuremberg, Cologne and many others—had similar enclaves of medieval and late medieval origin, preserved as islands of centuries-old survival amidst the regularly changing modernity hemming them about. And, until 1900, London, too, had such an enclave, and one which, today, would be a 'tourist trap' attracting visitors from all over the world.

The decision to demolish this surviving part of a London dating from as far back as Henry VI or Edward IV must be credited—if 'credited' be the right word?—to Frederic Harrison, the then chairman of the Improvements Committee of the London County Council. In 1892, Harrison added the 'Aldwych and Kingsway' proposal to the already agreed Strand Improvements Scheme, and eight years

Surprisingly, this squalid alley, Plummer's Court, was part of the vast slumland cleared away when Aldwych and Kingsway were built between 1901 and 1910

later the vandal-instructed workmen began to swing their picks. It is only recently that two of the Clare Market-type houses which stood on the south side of the Strand were demolished to make way for the extension to King's College, London University, a building in a style for whose deliberate ugliness I am quite unable to offer an explanation. To the west of King's College, past Somerset House (recently cleaned, and all the handsomer for it) is a row of four-storey houses with shops beneath. With the exception of the yellow-faience building (1899) at the corner of the Strand and Lancaster Place, and the new building of Gee & Co., next to Somerset House, all these houses are refronted seventeenth century buildings whose interiors—the upper storeys, of course—should be examined. The elaborate staircases, with their 'barley-sugar twist' balusters and the foliated consoles under the treads, bring back a world of gracious living, to use an apt American phrase, almost beyond our imagining.

I know of one other house in the Strand which hides a seventeenth-century interior behind an aggressively modern cement-rendered front. This is No 248 Strand, the shop of Dolland & Aitchison, the opticians. The great carved pine fireplace on the first floor, and the elaborate balusters on the third floor show clearly that this is merely a refronted house of Charles II's day. Behind it is Exchange Court, in which the Corps of Commissionaires has its headquarters, and to which the ex-sergeant of Royal Marine Light Infantry ('A Study in Scarlet') was attached.

Holmes and Watson also went east by road, along that Roman road which leads from Trafalgar Square to Mile End and beyond: through the Strand, up Cornhill, along Leadenhall Street, through Aldgate High Street and so along Whitechapel Road, either to continue straight on to Mile End or to branch off, 'half-right', at Gardner's Corner, to go along Commercial Road to Cubitt Town and the Isle of Dogs, where once Tudor monarchs coursed their racing hounds.

It was on 18 June 1887—the anniversary of the Battle of Waterloo, *and* in Golden Jubilee Year!—that an adventure took Holmes and Watson down to an East End which then retained much of a romantic gloom, as well as having the squalor it retains to this day.

They went, if you will recall, in connection with the singular disappearance of Mr Neville St Clair, whose wife had called on the professional services of Holmes in order to find her missing husband.

As Holmes remarked to Watson: 'I cannot recall any case within my own experience which looked at first glance so simple, and yet which presented such difficulties'. And, in addition to the inherent difficulties of the case, there are difficulties in Watson's narrative which have puzzled Sherlockians ever since the Higher Criticism began.

It was supposed that Neville St Clair had been foully done to death, but eventually Holmes tracked him down to a 'vile opium den, the Bar of Gold', whose location—since Watson's 'Upper Swandam Lane' does not exist—has so far defied the most ardent Sherlockian researchers. Mr St Clair, so he had told his wife and so his wife believed, was 'something in the City', a commuter living pleasantly at Lee in one of those half-acre-gardened villas which have now been cut up into flats or pulled down to make way for nasty little blocks of flats with 'twee' names.

But Neville, able to live in suburban comfort, if not (judging from Watson's description of the house in Lee) suburban luxury, was not exactly what his wife understood by 'something in the City'. He *was* something in the City—in fact, just what Mr Altamont, in Thackeray's tale was: a crossing-sweeper, whose gratuities, in pennies and halfpennies, kept the Lee establishment going, servant and all.

Pausing to reflect that muddy streets, necessitating the services of a crossing-sweeper, vanished only after the first World War, we might also consider the real or imaginary existence of that 'evil, Chinese' part of London—Limehouse and Pennyfields—description of which enabled the late Sax Rohmer and Thomas Burke to make a more than comfortable living.

To-day, the principal Chinese quarter of London is centred about Gerrard Street, which lies between Shaftesbury Avenue and Leicester Square. If one visits this old and now shabby street about tea-time on any weekday, one will find it crowded with Chinese of both sexes. There are Chinese restaurants, shops, clubs—even a strip-tease joint with, if not Chinese 'turns', at least Chinese posters flanking the front door. Many of these establishments have their fascias exhibiting only legends in Chinese; so restricted is their custom to the expanding Chinese population that they do not use English at all.

In Holmes's day—the day of the 'vile opium den' in fact or fiction —the London Chinese were concentrated about Pennyfields (sometimes spelt as two words, Penny Fields) and Limehouse Causeway, where to-day few are to be seen save in the very popular and by no means inexpensive Chinese restaurants which flourish there.

To find old London Chinatown, one takes the Commercial Road at Gardner's Corner, continues along the East India Dock Road at St Anne's Limehouse, and takes the West India Dock Road as it forks right. Here is Chinatown, consisting, says Clunn, of streets

> inhabited almost entirely by Orientals and (containing) foreign restaurants and drinking-shops hardly suitable for unaccompanied tourists. . . . Here the population consists of Chinese, Lascars, Maltese and a few Japanese. Here also one may dine in rather unusual but interesting surroundings on such Oriental delicacies as sea slugs, birds' nests and sharks' fins. Opium dens and fan-tan saloons still exist, despite the vigilance of the police, but it is not wise for the visitor to see these establishments from the inside.

These words, written in 1957, would have been valid in 1887 or even later, perhaps as late as 1920; they were hardly valid in 1957 and are completely inappropriate to the facts to-day. There *are* Orientals to-day in the East End of London, just as there are Orientals, and indeed persons from every part of the world, in every British city and town: it has been the policy of British Governments since about 1950 to see that this is so. The Asiatics and Overseas Home, built in 1857 for accommodating (principally) Lascars, is still in West India Dock Road, adjoining the London Seamen's Missions, so that one expects to find Asiatics in or near the Asiatics and Overseas Home. But the distinctive Chinese flavour of Limehouse and Pennyfields has gone. If, to-day, Nayland Smith were hunting down the infamous Dr Fu Manchu, the British Secret Service agent would not 'naturally' go East, to Pennyfields and Limehouse, but start looking for the Master of Evil a little nearer London's Clubland —say, in Gerrard Street, and, if that proved unfruitful, somewhat more to the West: perhaps in Park Lane or even off Knightsbridge.

Yet old memories cling about these parts. At the corner where the East and West India Dock Roads meet there is still the now rather dingy Eastern Hotel. Here, when on a visit to the East End, the then King of Siam, Chulalongkorn, sat down to a 'typically English luncheon' of brown Windsor soup, boiled plaice and anchovy sauce, roast beef and two veg., and what survives in the record as 'a sweet'.

With true Oriental courtesy, His Majesty declared himself enchanted with the Edwardian nosh, and decorated the landlord with the medal which had been specially brought along by the King's aide-de-camp.

Apart from 'vile opium dens', there was something east of London which must have engaged Holmes's attention on several occasions, even though the Canon preserves a perhaps discreet silence: the Tower of London.

Almost from the beginning of his practice as a private detective, Holmes had found himself operating at what we may call the 'high political level'. Royalty were amongst his earliest as they were amongst his most distinguished clients, and governments were not slow to follow where royalty led. Now, part of the mystique of 'government' is the myth that there are 'secrets', the betrayal of which is supposed to threaten the stability of the nation over which the 'betrayed' government has power. Holmes, like any other sensible man with his bread-and-butter to earn, played along with this absurd myth and zealously hunted down 'traitors' who had spoken out of turn. And traitors, then as well as now, went to the Tower, both whilst awaiting trial by a court held *in camera* and, should the verdict go against them, to meet their death by shooting in the grass-filled Tower moat.

Holmes, of course, did not mind the game of 'Hunt-the-Traitor'; it was only when, in order to make the game seem 'real', a 'traitor' had to be executed that Holmes let his true feeling for the law become apparent. In the case of 'The Naval Treaty' (Tuesday, 30 July to Thursday, 1 August 1889), Holmes was content to restore the missing treaty to Watson's old schoolchum, Percy Phelps, from whose desk in the Foreign Office it had been stolen; but there Holmes feels that his duty ends. He is content to let the thief go free; *not* to see that he is imprisoned, at best, or shot in the Tower, at worst. All the same, Holmes must have seen a lot of the Tower, even if only during those long hours of interrogation in which the accused is given every opportunity of incriminating himself.

The old statement that the Tower was first built by Julius Caesar has been, for some time now, rejected with scorn, but the truth is that if Julius Caesar did not establish a fort where the Tower now stands the original fort was certainly a Roman foundation, though, in its present form, the Tower is mainly Norman.

Of all the many 'sights' of London, there can be no doubt that the

Tower is the most popular, and to the credit of the management it may be said that, with the possible exception of the Zoological Gardens, no 'attraction' is better maintained or presented with a better appreciation of what the public likes to see.

The Crown Jewels and the splendid collection of ancient arms and armour in the Armoury would alone be sufficient to bring the crowds to nearby Tower (formerly Mark Lane) underground station, but the Tower has much more to offer to the visitor.

In its day it has been—and still, on occasion, is—a prison, and often elaborate memorials of their enforced stay left by prisoners from other centuries are not the least interesting of the Tower's sights. It was formerly a royal palace—officially, it still is—and it was from here that the sovereign spent the night before his or her coronation at Westminster, proceeding to Charing Cross (*not* to the Abbey) by barge along the populace-lined Thames. From Charing Cross, he or she would walk barefoot along 1,250 yards of blue cloth to the West Door of the abbey church of St Peter, where, on a 'scaffold', he or she would turn east, west, north and south, to show the people their rightful sovereign, whilst the heralds proclaimed the new monarch. Only then was the sovereign crowned.

It was here, too, in the ancient Tower, that the ambassadors of foreign countries were formally received, and it was here, too, that treaties of friendship and commerce were solemnly discussed and ratified.

It is a show, of course: the Tower has been that for centuries. But it is a show—Crown Jewels, Armoury, parading soldiers, Tudor-styled Beefeaters, axes, blocks and all the other grisly mechanisms of violent death, prisoners' despairing *graffiti,* ravens—played against a background whose sombre majesty has never been cheapened by the fact that sightseers have taken over from soldiers and statesmen and kings as the principal users of the Tower. It impresses even as it entertains.

The surroundings, too, of the Tower have improved greatly over the past century, and though the clearing of the approaches to the fortress involved the demolition of much that was picturesque, there is no doubt that the Tower looks all the better for the open ground to be found on all sides of it.

The clearing began with the removal, at the end of the last century, of a row of houses between Postern Row and George Street. This row of houses stood between Cooper's Row, a narrow street to the east of Trinity Square, and the Minories; the row was an obstruction to the free circulation of traffic and with its clearance the opening-up of the Tower approaches really began.

The bombing of the World War II accelerated the process, especially in demolishing the vast and ugly Myers warehouse—the 'Nightmare of Tower Hill'—which completely blocked out the sight of All Hallows Barking, beneath which lie the remains of a Roman temple of Mars Gradivus.

Unfortunately, a quarrel, or merely simple interdepartmental rivalry, between two government departments deprived London of the full benefit of one of war's 'good turns'—the exposure of an important piece of the Roman Wall on Tower Hill. One section of the exposed wall was in the 'care' of one government department; the other section in the 'care' of a different department. The first department carefully preserved 'its' section of London Wall; the second—not improbably out to be 'different from' its rival department—pulled down the wall in order, so their 'spokesman' said, to build a temporary urinal for the workmen engaged on demolishing bomb-damaged property in the vicinity.

However, what was preserved is well worth inspection, and there is another, and far better preserved, section of London Wall in nearby Cooper's Row. This was once in, and indeed formed the southern wall of, wine-vaults which, a century and more earlier, had been a workhouse; it is *said* that this was the workhouse to which 'Phiz' (Hablot K. Browne) went to draw the background for his immortal picture of Oliver Twist asking for more.

The wine-vaults of Joseph Barber have been pulled down and a little Kliptiko palace in the modern mode erected on their site, but the wall has been preserved. It is the longest section intact, and also the highest, with a sentry's walk of medieval origin and two arrow-slits of contemporary work.

It may be that Holmes visited the Tower some days after 2 August 1914, on which day he had tricked and arrested the German master-spy, Von Bork. As the Canon tells, Holmes and Watson took the German to London to hand him over to Inspector Stanley Hopkins, already, in view of the imminence of World War I, briefed for duty with the Special Branch. That Holmes felt that Von Bork's work in England deserved death seems to me to be evident from a brief

New Scotland Yard, as Holmes knew it. Opened in 1892 on the Embankment, it was extended to Parliament Street in 1912. To many, this will always be *the* 'Scotland Yard'

The new 'New Scotland Yard' on an important corner site formed by
Broadway (*left*) and Victoria Street (*right*). The dome in the centre of the
photograph is not an architectural feature of the new 'Yard' but belongs
to the Central (Methodist) Hall

conversation between the Sleuth of Baker Street and his eminent, if vile, captive.

> After a short, final struggle Von Bork was walked down the garden path and hoisted into the spare seat of the little car. His precious valise was wedged in beside him.
>
> 'I suppose you realise,' Von Bork snarled, 'that if your government bears you out in this treatment, it becomes an act of war.'
>
> 'What about your government and this treatment?' said Holmes, tapping the valise.
>
> 'You are a private individual. You have no warrant for my arrest. The whole proceeding is highly irregular.'
>
> 'Highly,' said Holmes.
>
> 'Kidnapping a German subject.'
>
> 'And stealing his private papers.'
>
> 'Well, you realize your position, you and your accomplice here. If I were to shout for help as we pass through the village ———'
>
> 'My dear sir, if you did anything so foolish, you would give the village a new public house, with "The Dangling Prussian" as its signpost. The Englishman is a patient creature, but his temper is a little inflamed at present. . . .'

From which it would appear that, though Britain and Germany were not yet officially at war, Von Bork's spying was to be dealt with at the highest and most severe, level. And that must have meant the Tower, with Holmes in constant attendance throughout the long interviews in which the Master Spy was interrogated with all that patient persistence for which both Special Branch and Military Intelligence (then already forty years old) have become justly famous.

Whether or not Von Bork was hanged—in which case he would have met his death at Pentonville—or executed by a firing squad—in which case the place of execution would have been the grassy moat of the Tower—Watson does not say. Perhaps Von Bork *did* chance a cry for help . . . in which case, Holmes's sinister threat may well have come true, with Von Bork's corpse dangling from an oak in one of these villages on the road from Harwich to London that not even petrol-pumps, the 'telly', or motorways have succeeded in modernising.

CHAPTER 6

Holmes Goes Down the Strand

Two centuries ago, the shops of the Strand were as renowned throughout Europe as were those of Cheapside, a mile or so to the east. The Strand was the most fashionable as well as the busiest street in London.

The glory has departed; to-day the Strand is not even a particularly busy street, since such shops as it has end more or less at Wellington Street and there is nothing to take the stroller further east once the shops have closed for the night. One good restaurant, Simpson's-in-the-Strand, and one first-class hotel, the Savoy, remain to remind the visitor that, fifty years ago or even less, this was *the* street of theatres and restaurants: Gatti's Royal Adelaide, Pratti's, the Vienna, Romano's, Haxell's, Horrex's, the Fountain, the Gaiety, the Cecil, the Golden Cross, the Grand Grill, and many others. Of the famous restaurants of the past, only Simpson's-in-the-Strand, the restaurants of the Savoy and Charing Cross Hotels, the Grand Grill and Rule's, in nearby Maiden Lane, still survive. The theatres I have already noticed, and there are still some left.

In Holmes's younger days, the Strand was considerably longer than it is to-day; that is, considered as a street along which Londoners and visitors would wish to perambulate. Until 1901, when the Kingsway and Aldwych 'improvements' began, the Strand ran from the corner of Northumberland Avenue on the south and Trafalgar Square on the north to Temple Bar (demolished and removed in 1878). It was a street consisting *only* of shops, hotels, restaurants and theatres, for the entrance gate to King's College

140

Having finished 'The Case of The Dying Detective' in 1889,
Holmes always a realist, remarked to Watson: 'When we
have finished at the police station, I think that something
nutritious at Simpson's would not be out of place.' Here is
Simpson's as it was in 1889, and as how it continued to be until
rebuilding in 1904. Holmes and Watson met there again in 1902
and must have continued to eat there after the rebuilding, when
the quality stayed the same, though prices went up

The Strand at the end of the last century, showing two establishments which must have been familiar to the friends: (*left*) Yates's Wine Lodge; (*right*) the Adelphi Theatre, which has since been rebuilt. During 'The Case of The Resident Patient,' Holmes and Watson strolled along the Strand, down Fleet Street and back for three hours

and the façade of Somerset House took up relatively little of two sides of a long street almost entirely devoted to entertainment.

The first great interruptions of the Strand's traditional frontages came with the building of the Royal Courts of Justice (1882) and, next door, the Law Courts branch of the Bank of England at the corner of Bell Yard and the Strand. Bell Yard incidentally, contains the oldest 'secret service' organisation in Britain: the Post Office's Investigation Department.

With the demolition of Dane's Inn, a picturesque former 'inn of court' in whose chambers journalists and other erratic persons lived cheaply and Bohemianly, and its replacement by offices, the north side of the Strand now terminated at the junction of Holywell Street and Wych Street. In 1901, Wych Street and all the other streets of Clare Market began to come down, and, with the construction of Aldwych and Kingsway, streets consisting mainly of offices, the 'shopping' part of the Strand ended at Wellington Street. The wide Strand frontage of the Cecil Hotel (opened 1899) included shops, many of them of a good class, as did the Strand frontages of the Savoy Hotel buildings (opened 1904), but further encroachment on the shopping area was effected by such 'non-shops' as Coutts's Bank, opened in 1902 on the site of the former Lowther Arcade, where the exiled Louis Philippe used to wander to ogle the pretty shop-assistants.

It is no slight to the existing Strand to say that the expensive shops, with the exception of The Savoy Taylors' Guild at the corner of Savoy Court, have left the thoroughfare. And with the extension of the front of King's College to cover the space between Surrey Street and the entrance to Somerset House, the shops of the Strand will be further severely diminished in number.

The search for good food and entertainment took both Watson and Holmes down the Strand; Watson, in fact, was living in a Strand private hotel, in 1881, when he met Holmes. We know that Holmes liked Simpson's, cheaper then than it is to-day, for Holmes could have lunched there in, say, 1890, or even much later, for half-a-crown; if all that he wished for were 'coffee, a good cigar and a game of chess', then he need have paid no more than a shilling. The theatres, too, of the Strand must have enjoyed both men's patronage, and perhaps the Prince of Wales, with something confidential to discuss, might have suggested to Holmes that he

Temple Bar, the gate which marked the western limits of the City of London. Removed to Theobald's Park, Hatfield, on the building of the 'new' Law Courts, it was not taken down until 1878, the year in which Holmes set up in practice. It must, then, have been familiar to him. Two or three of the early seventeenth-century houses adjacent are still standing; one (built 1629) is the well-known Wig & Pen Club

ask to be shown into one of the *cabinets particuliers* which in those days were a feature of Rule's restaurant in Maiden Lane.

Newspapers were familiar to Holmes; no fewer than twenty-one being mentioned by name in the record. Here is Fleet Street, then as now the centre of London's newspaper industry. Though extensively rebuilt, Fleet Street retains its old character in an astonishing way; perhaps because certain 'landmarks' such as 'Ye Olde Cheshire Cheese'—its sign can be seen on the left—are still a feature of 'the Street'

But since the Strand was and still is the main throughfare from the West End of London to the East End there were many other reasons apart from the desire to seek a restaurant or theatre which would have made the street and its continuations—Fleet Street, Ludgate Hill, Cheapside, Cornhill, and so on—familiar to Holmes.

The constant research, for instance . . .

Half-way down the Strand, on the south side, there was in 1880, and still is to-day, the greatest single repository of the kind of facts in which Holmes, professionally, had a primary interest. This is Somerset House, whose vast eighteenth-century elegance houses the Audit Office, the Inland Revenue Office (though the majority of its inherently proliferating departments have been moved elsewhere), the Wills Office and the headquarters of the Registrar General of Births, Deaths and Marriages, to whose files the public have easy though progressively costly access. With the exception of records concerning insolvency and crime—those we shall come to presently—most of the vital statistics of Great Britain since compulsory registration of births, deaths and marriages was introduced in 1837 are to be found at Somerset House. Its existence and constant employment are so taken for granted by Watson that he does not bother to enumerate the occasions on which Holmes stepped beneath the entrance arch, under the splendidly coffered vaults, and turned left, right or went straight on (depending upon what he was seeking), past the liveried servants who must always have given a respectful salute as they held open the door for the world's greatest private consulting detective.

Completely rebuilt by the great Scots architect, Sir William Chambers, in the decade after 1774, the former royal palace of Somerset House had become, after many vicissitudes, the home of the Royal Academy; and the inscriptions cut in the stone above the various record departments testify that it was for the Royal Academy that the palace was rebuilt. However, in the following century, the Royal Academy—collection and schools—was moved to the present National Gallery in Trafalgar Square until, in 1869, the Royal Academy found its permanent home in Lord Burlington's old Piccadilly mansion. The records of the nation were moved to Somerset House, the east wing having been given to King's College, founded 1828, and still in possession. This east wing was added only in 1824, so that, as an actual part of Somerset House,

Burlington Arcade, built in 1819. Badly damaged during World War II, it has been carefully restored to its old elegance and popularity. It stands next to the former mansion of the Earls of Burlington, to which the Royal Academy was transferred from Somerset House

its existence was brief—a mere four years. A separate doorway
for the College was constructed in the Strand, though in a style
not impressively harmonising with Chambers's work; this doorway
has recently been demolished as part of a new College front
which must surely stand, *primus inter pares,* as the ugliest erection
of a generation whose talent lies in the production of ugly buildings.

The west wing, fronting on Lancaster Place, is the work of the
Victorian architect, Sir James Pennethorne, and was not erected
until 1854-56. Whilst no slavish copy of Chambers's work, it
harmonises well with it and it is a pity that the Crown permitted
the small plot of land at the corner of Lancaster Place and the
Strand to become alienated; on it, in 1897, rose a building in the
ugliest type of Victorian *fin-de-siècle* commercial. If the entire
block could be used to complete the plans of Chambers and
Pennethorne (in their style, of course), London would have an
architectural masterpiece whose beauty would offset, to some extent,
the concrete horror which has risen the other side of Somerset
House.

A little further down the Strand, at the back of Dane's Inn (when
it was standing) or Clement's Inn, rebuilt in the 1880s as office
chambers, stood, until very recently, a Victorian stone building
whose grim appearance darkly shadowed forth the grim nature of
its function. This lump of heavy, soot-stained, Victorian govern-
ment-classic was Bankruptcy Buildings, which gloomed at the west
end of Carey Street. Inside it was even more dismal, and quite as
dirty, as outside; there was, indeed, something Dickensian in its
squalor: in every battered door and unswept corridor the building
seemed to say, 'No-one who could avoid it would ever come here
in the first place, so why make it attractive—seeing that its function is not to attract but to discourage visitors?'

Yet into its gloomy portals, and down its gritty stone stairs, past
the near-opaque windows which gave on to a dank garden full of
funereal laurel and holly and other such plants, Sherlock Holmes
must have gone many times. For all the insolvent debtors of
decades past are here: the honest ones, the dishonest ones, the
hopeful incompetents, and the sharp fellows who knew how to
capitalise themselves with a few adroit bankruptcies. Holmes
knew them all, and in the basement of Bankruptcy Buildings those

long, sensitive fingers which so impressed Watson must have turned many a dusty page in a battered file.

The old building is no more: a flash, streamlined office building now stands on the same site; but the rest of Carey Street has, so far, resisted change. On the south side are the back windows of The Law Courts, set amidst its spires, lantern and crocketed finials; here, not Caen stone, but bright red Victorian brick with stone dressings. In 1882, just after the completion of this magnificent structure by the son of the architect, G. E. Street, RA, who did not live to see his work finished, the inside of the building, especially the great entrance hall, must have looked very much as it does to-day, since the interior stonework has been cleaned—and most impressive the hall looks!

There are numerous courts in this palace of the Law, and it is not always easy to find one's way to the 'Bear Garden'—it seems to be a quasi-official name, since everyone, from attendants to learned counsel, uses it—or through the long corridors which become bridges over deep, booming halls whose floors are thirty feet below, and staircases climbing up and down, and odd little culs-de-sac lit by windows which *always* surprise with the unexpected view. And with every direction and every name carefully painted in a Victorian Gothic script which must have been devised for this building, for it is seen nowhere else.

It is easy to imagine Holmes, in the entrance-hall or in the 'Bear Garden', scrutinising the *Daily Cause List of the High Court of Judicature,* for though Holmes's rough-and-ready (and too often high-handedly autocratic) sense of justice prefers to avoid courts of law—in no fewer than ten of the Watson-reported cases does Holmes deliberately conceal a crime—he must often have been forced to go through the ordinary processes of law; the Scotland Yard men would have seen to that. Holmes cannot always have been able to do what he calls 'compounding a felony', but for which the more correct term (since Holmes was no qualified lawyer) is 'misprision of felony': concealing, not reporting, not punishing, a crime, in the interests of 'the higher justice'.

In the matter, for instance, of Lady Morcar's missing blue carbuncle, valued at £20,000, Holmes's rough-and-ready justice is willing to let the matter of punishment drop, seeing that the missing

Serjeants' Inn in 1890, by which time it had ceased to be the Inn of the
Order of the Coif, to which the serjeants-at-law belonged. It became a
place of chambers and offices, and though heavily bombed in World War
II, has been imaginatively restored

gem has been recovered undamaged. All the same, Holmes *does* excuse his illegal tolerance towards the thief: 'It is the season of forgiveness', he says to Watson. 'Chance has put in our way a most singular and whimsical problem, and its solution is its own reward . . .'

Barristers—there are not many in the Canon, and the only woman whom Holmes is known to have loved was probably not uninspired by malice when she eloped with one—can have liked Holmes as little as did the 'experts' of Scotland Yard: the latter were deprived of glory, the former of fees. In either case, there was ample justification for their having disliked Holmes intensely.

Every person born in England is, *ipso facto,* a member of the Church of England as by Law Established, whether or not that person be later baptised, and whether or not that person later be confirmed in the Faith.

Of course, the parents of many such persons have no wish to avail their children of this advantage; they wish the children to grow up Roman Catholics, Jews, Baptists, Methodists, Presbyterians, Congregationalists, Buddhists, Mahometans, worshippers of Shiva and the rest. The law makes allowance for this, but gives those who wish to be members of the Church of England one privilege not available to those who take their allegiance to another faith: the right to a special licence to marry, signed by, or on behalf of, the Archbishop of Canterbury.

Members of no other religion have this privilege: which brings me to 'Doctors' Commons', mentioned in 'The Case of the Speckled Band', and generally regarded—the mention, I mean—as a slip of Watson's pen.

Until 1867, there stood in Knightrider Street, between the present Queen Victoria Street and St Paul's Churchyard, Doctors' Commons, the old College of the Doctors of Law. The doctors lived here in collegiate style, dining together every Court day. When it was proposed to construct the new road joining the Mansion House to New Bridge Street—Queen Victoria Street—it was found that the new road would pass through the big, square garden of Doctors' Commons. On this, the doctors sold their property and divided the proceeds—as, a few years later, the Serjeants-at-Law were to do in Chancery Lane. The offices of the doctors, after having had some temporary lodgements in the interval, were eventually settled at the new Law Courts in the Strand. The Will Office, which had formerly been at Doctors' Commons, was transferred to Somerset House, where it still is.

What, then, did Watson mean when he said that Holmes had been to 'Doctors' Commons' to find a motive for the murderous Dr Grimesby Roylott's behaviour in the contents of a will by which Roylott would benefit in the event of his two stepdaughters' deaths? I suggest that, a mere fifteen years after the transfer of the Will Office from Doctors' Commons to Somerset House—the case of 'The Speckled Band' may be dated at 1883—Watson is using the term 'Doctors' Commons' in the sense merely of 'Will Office', as to-day we talk of various departments of Somerset House, even though these have been transferred to Bush House, Strand and Companies House, Old Street, St Luke's, two miles and more distant from Somerset House proper.

But, further to support the theory that Watson may not have been so incorrect after all, there is actually a Doctors' Commons—or, at least, the phrase—in current usage amongst London solicitors. I have heard it used of the department in the strange office building adjoining the Deanery to which application for Anglican special-licences must be made. If Holmes did not go to Doctors' Commons to find out the details of dead Mrs Roylott's will, then he might well have gone there—and, indeed, most certainly did—to obtain details of the special licences by which a number of persons of his acquaintance were married. One such was 'the Only Woman', Irene Adler, who was married to Mr Godfrey Norton, himself a barrister-at-law, by special licence. And the address of the Heralds' office is given as Doctors' Commons, as late as 1910.

The Deanery, spared during the bombing which hit St Paul's and destroyed the Victorian (but beautiful) baldacchino, is a charming little Charles II house, more like a country parsonage than the residence of the 'general manager' of a great cathedral. The Deanery was fortunate in that it was hidden away behind high brick walls, pierced by three panelled wooden gates, two for carriages and one for pedestrians. Had the Deanery been surrounded by iron railings, these would have been torn down in the 1940 'metal salvage drive' of dubious purpose and advantage; its privacy would have gone and, somehow or other, a 'reason' would have been found to alienate the ground thus exposed and opened to the public gaze. As it is, the old walls and thick wooden gates preserve this little oasis of old-fashioned peace in a London where privacy is mistrusted and attacked and there is little peace of any kind.

The great libraries of London are well known to scholars, but almost unknown to the ordinary book-borrower, who thinks that, apart from the reading room of the British Museum, if he has heard of this, or the similar reading rooms at Manchester and Liverpool, the local public library contains all that he is likely to need in the way of books. But even educated Londoners are unaware of the number and riches of the libraries which lie, mostly to the east of Charing Cross, open to the earnest researcher; libraries which were known to, and assiduously frequented by, Holmes, as he 'walked down the Strand'.

Bombing in World War II caused grievous losses in books and manuscripts, though modern scientific methods of restoration have achieved some astonishing results in recovering fire-damaged manuscripts. For instance, historic parchment manuscripts, locked in fireproof boxes at the Public Record Office, Chancery Lane, were so 'dehydrated' that a parchment several square feet in area had contracted to the size of a postage-stamp. (If the reader has inadvertently put a pair of chamois-leather gloves in too hot water, he will have some idea of what happens to parchment in the vicinity of a thermite bomb!)

Much of this war-damaged material has been restored to use; a triumph for the patient, unadvertised work of our libraries' 'preservation' staffs, who labour, at minimal salaries, for what can only be the love of their art.

But, in Holmes's younger days, accidents were still to be encountered, and certainly methods of keeping, filing, cataloguing, guarding, manuscripts and books were far inferior to those in use to-day.

Here are some of the libraries—among which I also include collections of factual documents of one sort or another—to which Holmes, both in his capacity of professional investigator and in his capacity of research-scholar, would have had access. Observe how many of them lie to the east of Charing Cross and even more to the east of Temple Bar.

Institute of Electricians (Now the Institution of Electrical Engineers), Embankment Gardens, WC2

Middle Temple, Temple, EC4

Inner Temple, Temple, EC4

Law Society, Chancery Lane, WC2

Public Record Office, Chancery Lane, WC2

Lincoln's Inn, WC2

St Mary-le-Strand, WC2 (Church records)

St Clement Danes, WC2 (Church records)

St Clement Danes School (Formerly in Houghton Street, where Holmes would have consulted the records)

St Dunstan-in-the-East, EC4 (Church records)

Temple Church, Temple, EC4 (Church records)

The Inns of Court Regiment (Devil's Own), Stone Buildings, Lincoln's Inn, WC2

Libraries of the various newspapers and magazines located in or about Fleet Street, too numerous to list here; but mention may be made of *The Daily Telegraph* (1857), *Morning Advertiser* (moved to Fleet Street, 1825), *Observer* (1791), *The Times* (1785), *Morning Post* (1774)

Records of the many insurance companies situate in Fleet Street, Chancery Lane, etc.

St Bride's Institute, Bride Lane, EC4 (One of London's 'unknown' treasures: free library, reading and lecture rooms, gymnasium, swimming-bath and classrooms for technical instruction!)

St Martin Ludgate (Church records)

St Paul's Cathedral (A library of unrivalled richness, many of whose documents have been transferred to the Guildhall Library)

The Deanery, St Paul's, St Paul's Churchyard

Records of the Minor Canons of St Paul's

The Guildhall Library, founded 1423, Gresham Street, EC3 (Contains City records which go back to the early days of Anglo-Saxon rule, with a specially fine collection of Roman relics)

The Bank of England (Includes a fine collection of Roman relics, mostly recovered from the site of the Bank itself)

The various private and joint-stock banks of Cornhill, Lombard Street, Threadneedle Street, Throgmorton Street, etc. (Though all the private banks and many of the joint-stock banks have been absorbed into the 'Big Four', their archivists maintain the old records with care and skill)

The various insurance companies around the Royal Exchange, some of them being very old: many date from the first half of the eighteenth century

With the exception of St Clement Danes School, which has now moved into the country (the London School of Economics having filtered into the vacuum left by the school's move), all the buildings or institutions mentioned in my list have survived the second World War. Where they were bombed, the damage has been repaired, and though, as in the case of the British Museum Library, filing and cataloguing are sadly in arrears, most of the information available to Holmes has been supplemented by more than fifty years of additional material, whilst improved methods of storage have made all information considerably more readily accessible.

Only when one begins to undertake research does one start to appreciate the quantity of material available to the researcher. The man who kept, as Holmes did, his own press-cutting library, can hardly have failed to know *every* source of information open to him in London.

Hunting up information on the Musgraves and the whereabouts of the ancient regalia of England, or casting a look over the more dubious aspects of City finance in the case of 'The Stockbroker's Clerk', Holmes, however immersed in his researches, must have had to break off occasionally to go from labour to refreshment. He was lucky in that his younger age was spent in a London so rich in eating-places of every type and of every price level that one could not possibly begin to list them outside of a book dedicated to them alone.*

Far too many of those that Holmes knew and visited have gone: victims of 'improvement', of 'development', of changing tastes and —perhaps most potent cause of all—contempt for the long-term, modest-profit venture, in whose running the customer, tradition and 'the connection' counted for more than taxable gain. But some

---

*The essentially Victorian entertainment of eating, especially eating out, is well described in *Victorian Entertainment,* by Alan Delgado, David & Charles, 1971.

Holmes and Watson were great patrons of Simpson's in the Strand. However, Holmes's frequent visits to the City must have made him familiar with this other Simpson's, still with its seventeenth-century charm, in an alley off Cornhill

remain, and some, too, that Holmes, on his visits to the Strand, Fleet Street, the Temple and the City, must have known well.

Pimm's, at the corner of Budge Row and Poultry is gone. It was a splendid establishment where everything was to be had, from caviare to a wonderful cream cheese, from oysters to Welsh rarebit, and where the famous Pimm's No 1 gin sling, served with borage sprouting its blue flowers from the dark pewter pint-pot, was to be tasted as nowhere else. The Pimm's in Bishopsgate, the Pimm's in Old Bailey—these, too, have gone; as has the wonderful Simpson's grill-room and chop-house in an alley at the back of Stoneham's bookshop in Cheapside—victims of a bomb in World War II.

There used to be, before the second World War, a chain of cheap but excellent restaurants in the old style: booths with green poplin curtains hung from brightly polished brass rods; flat-footed old waiters in greasy dress-coats, who, balancing six servings of 'cut-off-the-joint-and-two-veg' in each gnarled hand, would fly to serve with the speed of Atalanta on a spur of no more than tuppence or threepence. This was the Williamson's chain, of which only one remains, off Cheapside, but it is no longer a matter of a 'one-and-tuppenny' lunch. Times have changed, and prices with them.

There were hotels in the City and Strand in those days: Anderton's Hotel, in Fleet Street, with its palm-flanked promenade hall, in which, comfortable in basket-chairs, journalists and other topers drank in inexpensive comfort; Anderton's, before 1914, charged 2s a night, with service. And across the road, in Salisbury Square, was the vast Victorian Salisbury Hotel, whose building—it was latterly the London office of *The Times of India*—has not long given place to a modern office building.

Taverns and chop-houses that Holmes knew and patronised have either vanished, changed their identity beyond recognition or, saddest state of all, have lost that popularity which once made them household names.

There was a time, and it dated from the rebuilding of Ludgate Circus, in 1864, when 'The King Lud' under the arches of the Ludgate railway viaduct was world-renowned for the Welsh rarebit which smoked from early morning to late night on its free lunch counter. The Welsh rarebit, free or otherwise, has gone and, in all charity, we can say that 'The King Lud' is not today the best known of London's pubs.

'Ye Olde Cheshire Cheese', Mecca of the Fleet Street journalists and the American tourist, as it was in 1890, when only journalists knew it. Even Wine Office Court, in which this drawing was made, has hardly altered since

Across the road, from 'The Lud', was Shireff's Wine Lodge, a superior establishment whose excellent wares might have kept it popular to this day had a German bomb not gutted it in 1941.

There was, and is still, a Sweetings' restaurant at the corner of Queen Victoria Street and the middle part of Queen Street, City: lovers of oysters and smoked salmon still sit down in its carefully contrived 'homeliness', to which the never-by-any-chance-young aproned waiters make their own contribution. But the grand stone-fronted Sweetings' in Fleet Street—you may still see the name carved in the pediment—did not survive, and as 'The Falstaff' its career has been curiously chequered. It is no longer a pub.

'The Cheshire Cheese', of course, is still with us, as most American visitors know. In the early part of World War II, much of its seventeenth and eighteenth century interior was destroyed in a fire, caused not by an enemy bomb but by a fault in the electrical installation. It is to be regretted that the management did not see fit to replace the burnt panelling with something a little more costly than the present wall-covering.

By change of character and simple abolition, Fleet Street bars and taverns have known a sad diminution of number. Where, now, are the bars of Anderton's and the 'Salisbury'? Where are the 'Rainbow', the 'Mitre', the 'Bodega' in nearby Chancery Lane, the 'Devil', the old 'Cock'?* And all those taverns and wine-lodges—Davy's in Holywell Street was one of the most famous—in that liveliest of all London's 'fun places' now covered by the dreariness of Aldwych and Kingsway?

But what is left? Where, and what, are the surviving links between the then and the now? Where and what the places where one may eat and drink in the surroundings (though not, alas, at the same prices!) that Holmes and Watson knew?

One must allow for change and, in so allowing, one must remember that the fundamental changes which altered so many of London's popular drinking and dining establishments came within Holmes's day—came, in fact, at a time when Holmes was still relatively young.

Thus, for instance, Holmes was just fifty when the 'new' Simpson's-in-the-Strand opened in 1904, and when the Savoy Hotel

---

*Demolished 1886. A new 'Cock'—still surviving—was built on the opposite side of the road.

was greatly enlarged and extended from the Embankment (where it had been built in 1889) to the Strand. He was only forty-two when the Cecil—'the most magnificent hotel in Europe'—was erected on the Embankment, and only forty-five when it extended its premises to the widened Strand; the Strand façade, which includes a bar, is still standing, though the building has been converted to offices since 1930.

He was only sixty when the very superior Coburg Hotel, in Carlos Place, Mount Street, dropped the 'offensively German' name (the name of the British royal house, by the way, but in the 1914 wave of anti-German sentiment even 'German sausage' became 'breakfast sausage' and no-one would have dared to own a dachshund!) and adopted the present name of Connaught.

I have already commented on the disappearance of so many of the splendid cafés and café-restaurants which sprang up around and because of the widening of old or the construction of new streets—Shaftesbury Avenue, Charing Cross Road, the widened Strand, the widened Coventry Street, and the enlarged Piccadilly Circus. The Monico has vanished, the Popular (1896) in Piccadilly, is now the offices of Transworld Airways, the Trocadero is now a dance-hall (as was, curiously, the old, notorious Argyll Rooms on whose site the 'Troc' rose in 1896), and the bars of the Pavilion exist no more. But Claridge's, the Criterion, the Café Royal, the Savoy, Simpson's-in-the-Strand, the 'George and Vulture', Simpson's (Cornhill), the Jamaica Winehouse (at Michael's Alley, Cornhill), Birch's (moved from Cornhill to New Broad Street, 1926, but since moved to Angel Court, Throgmorton Street)—all these that Holmes knew well are still with us. And there are other places, more private, of course, which have survived with so little change that one marvels to hear the phrases 'fundamental social trends' and 'complete revolution in our society' mentioned in their surroundings. I refer to those bastions of the Good Life: the City livery companies (at whose head is the Lord Mayor) and the four Inns of Court.

Some of the magnificent halls of the livery companies were either seriously damaged or completely destroyed during World War II, but most have now been rebuilt, their treasures taken out of safe-keeping, and their liverymen free to entertain once more in the lavish style for which 'City hospitality' has been famous for centuries.

The Mansion House, official residence of the Lord Mayor of London. Built on the site of the ancient Stocks Market, the Mansion House was designed by George Dance, the City Surveyor, the foundation stone being laid on 25 October 1739. The two upper storeys of Dance's original design had to be removed in 1840 as they were endangering the stability of the building. Almost every well-known person in the world has come to this fine old building as a guest over the past two-and-a-half centuries

It is my opinion that many, if not all, of the City's livery companies descend in a direct line from the trade-guilds or religious 'colleges' of Roman London: certainly the Vintners' peculiar fillets are identical in pattern with some Roman religious fillets found in York and now on display in the British Museum. The elaborate and ancient ritual with which these livery companies conduct their business should not blind the anti-traditionalist into thinking that their members are 'playing at antiquity', as I have heard it expressed. London, though deprived of its parliamentary representation by political and class prejudice of the most obnoxious kind, is still ruled internally by the livery companies, the majority of whose members are self-made business successes. Sir Polydore de Keyser, whose De Keyser's Royal Hotel stood on the Embankment at Blackfriars where Unilever House now stands, came to England as a penniless Belgian waiter and stayed to become lord mayor of what was then the greatest city in the world.

Much of the power has passed from the liveries, but he would be mistaken who would affirm that *all* power has passed. And even if it had, the riches of the liveries, accumulated over centuries of London's commercial world dominance, still remain: they keep schools going, they contribute largely to other charities, and they maintain, in a world of ever-falling standards, the ideals of the Good Life: their banquets are never notable for austerity. Even if Holmes might have felt the going a little too rich, Watson, we may be sure, would have tucked into the aldermanic plenty.

Rivalling the liveries in riches and a traditionally obstinate refusal to lower their standards in a standard-lowering society, come the Inns of Court, whose benchers lunch and dine no less comfortably than they did when Evelyn and Pepys, Lamb and Dickens, grew round-eyed at the splendour of the benchers' plate-laden tables.

And here Holmes was far more likely to come than to the gut-swelling aldermanic spreads: no man so intimately concerned with crime and punishment could have failed to become intimate with important members of the four Inns of Court. Many an invitation from the benchers of all four must have come the way of Holmes and Watson, for, next to food, the benchers love extending their hospitality—perhaps from a subconscious desire to prove that the stern, bewigged personification of Justice is far more human than even the ordinary man. Over the centuries, the various royal families of England and Scotland, Wales, France and, since 1603, Great Britain, have been entertained in these still surviving halls. Not only food and drink, all of the best, have been poured out by the generous benchers for their distinguished guests, but lavish entertainment, too. In the armorially-decorated hall of the Middle Temple, a Gothic structure built in 1572*, a barrister of the Middle Temple, named Manning, wrote this in his diary on 2 February (Candlemas) 1602, before going to bed that night:—

> At oure feast we had a play called *Twelfe Night,* or *What you Will,* much like *The Comedie of Errours* or *Menechnie* in Plautus, but most like and neere to that in Italian called *Inganni.*

Even today, with all their sophistication, the benchers do not entertain their guests with a first performance of a Terence Rattigan or Arthur Miller play—and Shakespeare was very much

---

*Bombed in World War II, but carefully and well restored.

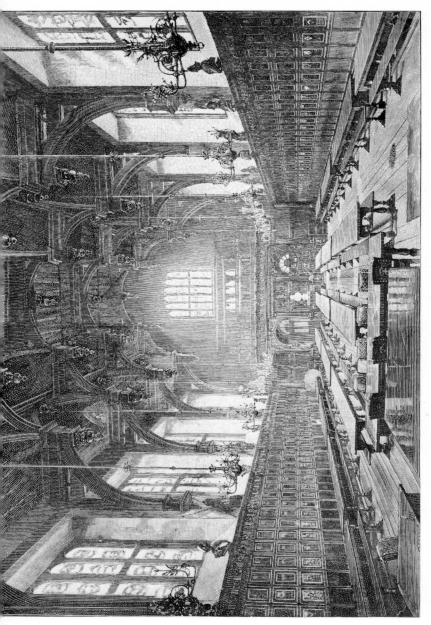

Middle Temple Hall, built in 1572, with a splendid hammer-beam roof made of oak, reputedly taken from Spanish galleons. Badly bombed during World War II, its restoration is a tribute to what money and craftsmanship can do in efficient partnership. It was here, on 2 February 1602, that Shakespeare's *Twelfth Night or What You Will* was first staged *the* great dramatist by 1602 when the benchers produced, for the first time, his *Twelfth Night*.

I have pointed out elsewhere that songs sung in the Middle and Inner Temple 'moots' are to be found in Shakespeare. That there was an intimate connection between him and the Inns of Court is obvious, and he may even have been an honorary bencher, as Sir Francis Drake was.

Some years ago, when I was dining at the Ambassadors Club, one of my fellow-guests was the professor of mercantile law at the University of Madrid. He expressed a desire to see over one of the four Inns of Court; more particularly, he wished his son to see how the English legal system was directed. Through the kindness of Mr Commissioner John Latey, QC, this was arranged, and Mr Latey, who was then the treasurer of the Middle Temple, most courteously conducted my guests and me through those back parts of the Middle Temple where even junior barristers are in *terra incognita*.

Now the benchers, who may be called the 'directors' of an Inn of Court, divide their meals into several stages; in the Middle Temple there are four stages, each being taken in a different room.

Food plays an important part in the ritual of English law; so much so that a law student, even though he has taken his bar finals, will not—indeed, cannot—be 'called to the bar' until he has 'eaten his dinners'; that is to say, has attended twelve dinners in his inn's own hall.

The benchers take the first part of their meals in hall, separated from and raised above students and other lesser mortals. They then leave the hall and retire into a set of chambers, all of the greatest comfort, in which they take the rest of their meal, ending up in the third inner room for their port.

At some point in our peregrination—it was not the hour of dinner, and we had the inner rooms to ourselves—Mr Latey drew my attention to a heavy table of late Elizabethan or early Jacobean manufacture.

'Your friends', he said, 'might be interested in this table. It is made from wood from the *Golden Hind*'.

"Indeed', I said. 'Drake's ship. Sir Francis Drake', I added, pronouncing the name in the Spanish manner.

'Ah, si! Francisco Drákè!' said the Professor. 'Si . . . el pirato!'

Well, it all depends on which history-book one reads: Drake, John

Paul Jones, Surcouf . . . they were all 'pirates' to the other side.

We were now in what is called 'the Parliament Chamber' to which repair the benchers to deal with port and dessert in the privacy that their rank has earned them. Dickens talks of the 'blue-nosed, bulbous-shoed old benchers in select port wine-committee assembled after Hall', but then he was looking at matters from the prejudiced view of one who had dined in hall only as a student.

A view of a meal in hall impresses by its 'formal-informality'; there is no such elaborate ritual as is found, for instance, in similar gatherings of a City livery company. Everyone present is robed according to his or her degree, and it is a convention in the Middle Temple that women students shall sit together. The treasurer and benchers sit at a long table on the dais, the barristers below them at the seniors' table; the students filling the body of the hall. The waiters, from their ancient association with bread, are here known as 'panyers', and grace is announced by the senior panyer's banging on a book (not The Book). All but the benchers are divided into separated 'messes' and to each 'mess' a set quantity of wine is allocated. In the days when religious taboos were more strictly kept than they are today, the presence of a Mohammedan or other abstainer was eagerly welcomed in any 'mess', for it meant that his portion went to his fellow diners.

It is noteworthy that those who have criticised the benchers—I quoted Dickens above, and one recalls that Lamb more than once spoke of them as 'slipshod'—were never of their select company. Entry to the Parliament Room might have modified those prejudices.

It is less formal now than it was even in Holmes's younger days, but even then dinners in hall were very tame affairs compared with the tuck-ins of the sixteenth century, when the diners were summoned by 'the reports of cannon', and at every course of the dinners trumpeters 'blew a courageous blast', whilst, during the meal the diners were entertained with the music of 'violins, shakbuts, cornets and recorders'.

That, with the ritual dancing which punctuated and ended each dinner, has gone; but on Grand Nights much of the old splendour is recalled, when distinguished guests sit at the high table and a special menu does honour to the culinary traditions of the Law.

One should make a point of visiting the four Inns of Court, even though one may never receive an invitation to dine in hall or take port in the Parliament Room. All but a few portions of the Inn date from the late seventeenth century, for the disastrous fire of 1644, followed by the greater fire of 1666, and, so far as the Temple was concerned, another serious fire some twenty years later, removed almost all the remains of the medieval monastic building that the lawyers had inherited when the Order of the Temple was abolished in the early fourteenth century.

Much rebuilding in Victorian 'Gothic' has failed to destroy the essentially later Caroline character of the Inns, and it is to be noted with pleasure that modern rebuilding, necessitated by the bombing of World War II, follows the seventeenth and not the nineteenth century styles. The rebuilding of the Master's House in the Inner Temple has been well done indeed: it was a charming little house in the Dutch style of William III, and, completely destroyed by a bomb in 1940, it has now risen again to enchant us with its simple beauty.

All the Inns of Court, being in the centre of London, were damaged, to a greater or lesser degree, by the bombing, but all have now been restored and, here and there, improved. All are easily accessible to the visitor, and each retains in its unpretentious domestic architecture the tradition of an age far richer than ours in those human qualities which make for the stable society.

But there is one place of refreshment connected with the Law that Holmes and Watson cannot have avoided, and which is open to every member of the public who cares to walk along the Strand, take the District Railway to Temple Station, or any bus which stops at the Law Courts. This is The Crypt, recently 'modernised' and so deprived of much of its antique charm, but still well worth the visit, even though the food has been 'modernised', too.

The Crypt is rather more than its name implies. True, it *is* a crypt. as Gothic (and now as gloomy) as though it dated from 1282 and not merely from 1882; it is, in fact, the crypt of the Royal Courts of Justice that we noticed previously. For nearly a century now, it has been known to generations of litigants, witnesses, counsel, solicitors, law clerks, pettifoggers and those rootless hangers-on of the Law that every country and every age knows, as 'The Crypt'. It opened with the main building, as a refreshment-room, and in more ample days than this it served a reasonably good meal—

something counsel always seemed to be able to eat, but their clients rarely.

There was a long and rather grubby bar, at which the drinks ordered served as a pretty accurate index of the orderer's state of mind: bitter-beer for those who had nothing to do or nothing to fear; stronger stuff for the shaky of argument and shaky of hand.

In any lawsuit which lasted longer than a few minutes or which necessitated no more than one's going into the Law Courts, making an appearance in court, and leaving immediately one's evidence had been taken, a visit to The Crypt was, to use an outdated legal expression, a *sine qua non*. Holmes *must* have been in The Crypt, and on far more than one occasion.

One wonders what he ate there. The 'cut off the joint and two veg' at a shilling? A mere 'cup of tea and Bath bun' at three-halfpence? Or some of that brandy that Watson was so fond of pouring down other people's throats? If so, Holmes would have paid 3d for what, today, would be considered a quite generous measure.

CHAPTER 7

'Decorations Will Be Worn'

Holmes, like so many people who have not been 'brought up to money', was ambivalent in his attitude towards it; he liked it, he liked to have it, but he was nervous of mentioning it. He liked to pretend that he did not need it, and when it had to be mentioned, Holmes (though he may not have been aware of this) embarrassed others by the roundabout way in which he would first affect to refuse and then permit himself to be coaxed into accepting his fee—honestly earned and as honestly offered. Some fool has speculated somewhere that Holmes might have been a lawyer. This is rubbish. No lawyer would have been embarrassed in mentioning money, backward in claiming his fee, or hesitant in forcing the debtor to disgorge.

But Holmes was recompensed in other ways than in monetary payments; indeed, considering Holmes's reluctance to get down to business when it came to discussing cash, it was often probably found more convenient to both sides to discharge Holmes's claim by a payment which would not affect his touchy middle-class money-consciousness. A royal person or a government official would have been in a most advantageous position to respect Mr Holmes's sensitivity: an order or title would have been the ideal (and ideally acceptable) substitute for 'embarrassing' money.

For, though, as recorded by Watson in 'The Adventure of the Priory School', Holmes had so overcome his reluctance to charge expensively that he collected a £6,000 fee from the Duke of Holdernesse for having found his missing heir, Holmes must have profited, *financially,* far less than his talents and fame would have made probable, seeing that he continued to inhabit the apartments at Baker Street, that he had chosen in the days of his near-poverty. It is a point worth bearing in mind. True, Watson and Holmes improved their condition: ordered new furniture, laid in stocks of liquor, and hired a lad in buttons. But the rooms were the same. Holmes must have sacrified a lot of money to his middle-class eccentricity of pretending to be 'of independent means'.

How, then, was he otherwise recompensed? By what the formal invitation means when, at the bottom of the card it says, in discreetly small characters: 'Decorations will be worn'.

So far as I know, this is the first attempt to enumerate the 'decorations' that Holmes *most probably* was awarded, for services which, as we noted in chapter 4, were rendered to many of the royal families of Europe; and, if Mr Baring-Gould's surmises are correct, to the then ruler of Thibet.

But, without too much speculation, let us see if we may list the persons or states to which Holmes rendered acknowledgeable service. (This extends the list on page 36.)

In preparing this list, we have to take into account not only Watson's gratuitous 'tact' in 'concealing' true names under rather clumsy pseudonyms, but—we must admit it—Watson's own unfamiliarity with the greater world in which his distinguished friend moved. We shall, in preparing this list, have to make a few explanatory adjustments to the Watsonian text.

    1. 'The King of Scandinavia'. (Some time between March 1881 and October 1886.) As the heir to the *Swedish* throne bears the title, 'Duke of Scandia', I think we may take it that Watson is here talking of the king of what was then the dual kingdom of Norway-Sweden, Norway not having separated from Sweden until 1905. The King of Sweden, in 1881-6, was Oscar II, son of Napoleon I's marshal, Jean-Baptiste Bernadotte, who ascended the throne of Sweden as King Christian VII. Watson, however, is correct when he refers to Holmes's services to the King of Scandinavia as 'a delicate case'.

    2. 'The service for Lord Backwater'. We have no details of this case, which must, again, have occurred between March 1881 and October 1886. But the (obviously Watson-

concocted name of 'Backwater' reminds one so irresistibly of the 'Backs' at *Cambridge* that one feels that, under the name of Lord Backwater, Watson is concealing the identity of the Duke of Cambridge, grandson of George III, a cousin of the Queen and Commander-in-Chief of the British Army. In this case, the Duke's powerful influence would have been sufficient to induce the Government (or Sovereign) of the day to reward Holmes with a decoration—we know that he refused a title even as late as 1902.

3. Services to the British Government:
   a. 'The Adventure of the Second Stain', October 1886.
   b. 'The Second Adventure of the Second Stain', July 1889.
   c. 'The Naval Treaty', July 1889.
   d. 'The Third Adventure of the Second Stain', before December 1889.
   e. 'The Adventure of the Bruce-Partington Plans', November 1895.
   f. (*Perhaps*) 'The Shocking Affair of the Dutch Steamship *Friesland*', April-December 1894.
   g. 'The Case of the Two Coptic Patriarchs', July 1898.
   h. *His Last Bow*—the frustrating of Von Bork, Sunday, 2 August 1914.

4. Services to the United States Government:
   a. 'The Dreadful Business of the Abernetty Family of Baltimore', Tuesday, 6 July 1880.
   b. *The Valley of Fear*, January 1888.
   c. (*Perhaps*) 'The Very Abstruse and Complicated Problem Concerning the Peculiar Persecution of John Vincent Harden, the Well-Known Tobacco Millionaire', April 1895.
   d. 'The Case of the Ferrers Documents', early May 1900.
      NB. This case is merely referred to by Watson in 'The Adventure of the Priory School', and was never recounted by him. No papers were reported missing by the 10th Earl Ferrers from either of

his seats, Staunton Harold, Ashby-de-la-Zouch, or Chartley Castle, Stafford. The papers, then, involved another important branch of the Ferrers family, and since Sherlock Holmes interested himself in the matter, they can have involved only the most famous 'Ferrers' of them all: George Washington, Father of the United States of America. Washington was descended from Robert de Ferrers, 8th and last Earl of Derby, a title created in 1138. What Watson calls 'the Ferrers Documents' must have been part of the Washington archives, carefully preserved in the republic that Washington did most to create. Were the papers stolen? And why? To discredit Washington, by destroying the authentication of his gentle birth? It seems to me that this is one of Holmes's cases which deserves far more investigation than, so far, it has received.

5. Services to the French Government:
   a. 'The French Will Case', September 1888.
   b. 'The Matter of Supreme Importance to the French Government', late December 1890—March 1891.
   c. (*Almost certainly for the French Government*) Holmes conducted researches into the coal-tar derivatives at a laboratory in Montpellier. For high-explosives—or poison-gas?
   d. 'The Tracking and Arrest of Huret, the Boulevard Assassin', between April and December 1894. Mr Baring-Gould suggests that Huret was out to assassinate the President of the French Republic —assassination was popular in the decade 1890-1900—and I think that Mr Baring-Gould may well be right in his surmise.

6. Services to the Dutch Government:
   a. 'The Delicate Affair of the Reigning Family of Holland, November 1886—January 1887.
   b. 'The Netherland-Sumatra Company and the Colossal Schemes of Baron Maupertuis', February—early April 1887.

Clubland in Holmes's day. (*Above*) Arthur's Club, named after a keeper of White's Chocolate House, who died in 1761; (*Below*) Brooks's Club, named after its first proprietor, an eighteenth-century wine-merchant and money-lender. Both these smart St James's clubs have weathered the changes of fashion and taste of over two centuries. The club to which Holmes's brother, Mycroft, belonged, was in nearby Pall Mall, handy for Mycroft's chambers in the same exclusive street

   c. *(See* 3 f above). 'The Shocking Affair of the Dutch Steamship *Friesland*', April-December 1894.

7. Services to the Sublime Porte:
   a. 'The Commission for the Sultan of Turkey', January 1903.
8. Services for the Imperial Russian Government:
   a. 'The Summons to Odessa in the Case of the Trepoff Murder', November 1886—January 1887.
9. Services to the Vatican:
   a. 'The Little Affair of the Vatican Cameos', late April—early May 1888.
   b. 'The Famous Investigation of the Sudden Death of Cardinal Tosca', May or June 1895.
10. Services to the British royal family:
   a. *(Perhaps*—see 2, above) 'The Service for Lord Backwater', March 1881—October 1886.
   b. 'The Saving of Colonel Prendergast in the Tankerville Club Scandal', before September 1887.
   c. *(Perhaps* a royal connection—and so the need for Holmes's discretion in) 'The Red-Headed League', October 1887. I do not think that Holmes's involvement with this case *originated* with the royal family, but at some time during 'this rather fantastic business' he remembered that the swindler, John Clay, was the by-blow of a royal duke. It was Golden Jubilee Year, remember, and the Radical newspapers would have made much of a royal (even though illegitimately royal) con-man.
   d. 'The Blackmailing Case', September 1888. Watson makes no further mention of this case; there are *no* details. From the very reticence of the record, I am inclined to think that this case involved the royal family.
   e. *(Almost certainly)* 'The Atrocious Conduct of Colonel Upwood in Connection with the Famous Card Scandal at the Nonpareil Club', October—November 1888. I fear that this involved the Prince of Wales, who was to be involved, a year or so later, in a much more publicised card

scandal.

f. 'The Services Which May Perhaps Some Day Be Described', early June 1902. That this was the year of the ending of the Boer War and of the (delayed) coronation of King Edward VII makes it certain that the 'services' so discreetly mentioned by Watson were rendered, not to the British government, but personally to the royal family.

NB. That there were perhaps many other occasions on which Holmes's unique gifts were called upon by the royal family is evident from the gift of a costly emerald tie-pin and by the offer of a knighthood, the latter gift being refused.

11. Services to the Imperial German Government:
(*Probably* more than the single case of) 'The Saving of Count von und zu Grafenstein', before October 1903.

These are the principal cases, mentioned in the Canon, which involved governments or royal families. It must not be forgotten that the royal family of Scandinavia (Sweden) returned to Holmes for help at least twice, in late December 1890 ('The Service for the Royal Family of Scandinavia') and in early July 1895 ('The Summons to Norway'). That summons could only have come from the King of Sweden, then gravely disturbed by the movement for the separation of Norway from Sweden, which partition did, in fact, take place without bloodshed, though not without bitterness, in 1905.

I have to add one last item, but it stands by itself because it is still not clear just whom Watson is referring to when he talks of 'the Hereditary King of Bohemia'—Baring-Gould stoutly maintains that it was the Prince of Wales. However, let us add:

12. Services to the Kingdom of Bohemia:
'A Scandal in Bohemia', May 1887.

Now let us see which orders and decorations all this successful activity on behalf of governments and royal families must certainly have earned Holmes—remembering, too, that royal personages in those days were far more generous in bestowing such rewards than they have since become under 'liberal' governmental thinking.

To sum up the known royal families and governments on whose bounty, in the matter of orders or decorations, Holmes had a

Is this photograph of King Edward VII when Prince of Wales confirmation of the late Baring-Gould's theory that the so-called 'Hereditary King of Bohemia' in 'A Scandal in Bohemia' was, in fact, the Prince of Wales? On appearances alone, the theory would seem to have some substance

legitimate claim, may we make the following list:

The Royal Family of Great Britain
The Government of Great Britain
The Royal Family (especially the King) of Scandinavia (ie Sweden)
The Government of the United States
The Government of the French Republic
His Holiness the Pope (Leo XIII)
The Government of the Roman States (ie the Vatican)
The Royal Family of Holland (especially King William III)

The Government of the Dutch Kingdom
The Sultan of Turkey (Sultan Mohammed V)
The Government of the Sublime Porte
The Imperial Russian Government
The 'Kingdom of Bohemia'
The Coptic Patriarchate of Alexandria

—fourteen sources of honours referred to in the Canon; though, of course, this list cannot comprise the whole of those potencies for whom Holmes worked. At a levée in St James's Palace, at a Mansion House dinner, or at a royal reception to some visiting monarch who had expressed a particular wish to meet, or to meet again, 'the greatest detective in the world', Holmes's coat must have glowed with multi-coloured enamels, blazed with gold and silver, coruscated with diamonds, rubies and all the other less self-effacing gems. It is a pity that Sidney Paget, who has given us Holmes in 'shortie' covert coat, long travelling coat, morning coat (with 'come-to-Jesus' collar), short jacket, dressing gown, and with hats of an immense variety, did not sketch the Master in court dress of blue velvet and black silk, with cut steel buttons and dress sword, cockaded hat under his left arm. And, naturally, his left breast ablaze with orders and decorations.

Can we make a guess at which orders must have sparkled on Holmes's breast? I think we can. Bearing in mind that Holmes as (*a*) a foreigner, and (*b*) a non-Catholic, would have been excluded from certain orders abroad, here is the most likely list I have been able to compile:

Country/Monarch	Order/Decoration
* NB. As Holmes had refused a knighthood, no order of chivalry to which he was admitted (in Great Britain, that is to say) would have graded him above the rank of Companion or Commander, since the grade next highest would have carried a knighthood with it.	
HM The Queen	Companion (Civil), the Most Honourable Order of the Bath. CB.
	Commander, the Royal Victorian Order (after 21 April 1896). CVO.
HM King Edward VII	The Order of Merit, instituted 1902 by King Edward VII to re-

	ward those of his subjects who wished for no title. This Order may well have been instituted for Holmes himself. OM.
The British Government	Companion, the Most Distinguished Order of St Michael and St George. CMG.
The King of Sweden	Grand Cross, the Order of the Seraphim. Grand Cross, the Order of the Polar Star.
The United States of America	Commander, Legion of Merit.
The French Government	Commander, Legion of Honour. Les Palmes Academiques. Chevalier, Ordre du Mérite Agricole. (For Holmes's work at Montpellier in 1893-4)
His Holiness the Pope	Cavaliére, Order of St Gregory the Great.
The Vatican	Commendatore, Order cf the Holy Sepulchre.
The King of Holland	Chevalier, Order of the Marguerite
The Dutch Government	Chevalier, Order of Orange-Nassau.
The Sultan of Turkey	Chevalier, Order of the Medjidieh.
The Turkish Government	Chevalier, Order of Nishan-Iftikah.
The Imperial Russian Government	The Order of St Anne, 2nd class. Chevalier, Order of St Andrew. (This order was open only to those who already belonged to another Russian order; Holmes's membership of the Order of St Anne opened the Order of St Andrew to him.)
The Coptic Patriarchate of Alexandria	The Order of St George.

| 'The Hereditary King of Bohemia' | As the 'kingdom of Bohemia' was *en disponibilité* in 1887, Holmes's royal client almost certainly made him a member of the Cassel-Falstein family order: the Order of the Black Lion. Much as Holmes appears to have disliked the King's character, he was not averse to accepting a token of the royal gratitude. He accepted a snuff-box of old gold with a huge amethyst in the lid; Holmes, then, would have accepted membership of 'the King's' family order. |

This, in my opinion a most conservative list, shows that Holmes had *at least* nine decorations or orders; in all probability had as many as nineteen, and could well have had twenty or more. Taking into account the fact that he helped the same royal family or government more than once, and that kings and prime ministers would have passed Holmes on to 'friendly' monarchs and politicians, Holmes can hardly, in 1920 say, have failed to have been the holder of more than thirty of such sought-after distinctions.

However, let us assume that the list as I have given it represents the total of his honours; to which, of course, must be added the emerald tie-pin from Queen Victoria. Where would Holmes have gone to receive these honours, to have them hung around his neck or pinned to his breast, with a congratulatory word from the Fount of Honour or his or her accredited representative?

For the British honours, Holmes would have gone to Windsor Castle or Buckingham Palace, depending upon which royal residence the Queen was then favouring. Though Victoria held her Court at both Holyroodhouse and Balmoral, and sometimes even at Osborne House, Isle of Wight, investitures were almost always held at Windsor or (more frequently) at Buckingham Palace. Sometimes, though, the Queen, when she was specially desirous of showing her personal satisfaction for loyal services splendidly rendered, would decorate a subject at a private investiture: Holmes may well have been commanded to one of these private ceremonies.

As for the other orders and decorations, he would probably have

Osborne House, Queen Victoria's seaside palace and one to which she was especially devoted because it had been designed and lived in by her dead husband the Prince Consort. An easy run from London, it must often have been visited by Holmes. The photograph below shows the elegance of the interior. The marble statue is of the sentimental Queen's favourite dog: the British royal family is consistently attracted to music, dogs and horses (and not necessarily in that order!)

received them in London, at the legation or embassy of the nation concerned; to receive them again at the personal investiture, by monarch or president, when next Holmes was in the country where the honour originated.

Assuming, then, that Holmes received his honour in London, he would have attended the following to receive them. Choosing an 'average' date, I have selected the year 1892 as that in which Holmes might have been summoned to the various embassies and legations. In different years, of course, there were different envoys and different addresses; the year 1892 is, however, 'average'.

Sweden-Norway. Legation: 52 Pont Street, SW. (The legation had moved shortly before 1892 from Chesham House, Chesham Place, Lowndes Square, SW.) Envoy Extraordinary and Minister Plenipotentiary: Monsieur Akerman.

United States of America. Legation: 31 Lowndes Square, SW. Envoy Extraordinary and Minister Plenipotentiary: Robert Todd Lincoln, the rather unattractive son of President Lincoln, and recalled by the State Department because of his inability to charm the British.

Republic of France. Embassy: Albert Gate House, Hyde Park, SW. Ambassador: Senator William Henri Waddington.

Papal See. (There was no Papal Nuncio in Britain, and the office of Apostolic Delegate, ie, diplomatic representative, was 'vacant'. Holmes would almost certainly have been invited to receive his Papal decoration(s) from the Archbishop of Westminster: His Eminence Cardinal Henry Edward Manning, at Archbishop's House, Carlisle Place, SW. A new Archbishop's House was built in Ambrosden Avenue a few years later, and Cardinal Manning's old house is now the (very well kept-up) office of Humphreys & Glasgow Ltd, the international constructional engineers.

The Netherlands. Legation: 40 Grosvenor Gardens, SW. Envoy Extraordinary and Minister Plenipotentiary: Count van Bylandt.

Turkey. Embassy: 1 Bryanston Square, W. Ambassador Extraordinary and Minister Plenipotentiary: Rustem Pasha. (Rustem Pasha, though a Turk, was also a Christian, and though, of course, perfect in the diplomatic language of

French, was also very fluent in English, which made him popular in the society of the 1890s.)

Russian Empire. Embassy: Chesham House, Chesham Place, SW. (Acquired from the Swedish.) Ambassador Extraordinary and Minister Plenipotentiary: Monsieur G. de Staal.

Coptic Patriarchate. There was a representative of the Khedive of Egypt in London, but the Coptic order confered on Holmes would almost certainly have been presented to him by a senior official of the Foreign Office, in Whitehall, SW.

German Empire. Embassy: 9 Carlton House Terrace, SW. Ambassador Extraordinary and Minister Plenipotentiary: Count Hatzfeldt-Wildenburg. It was to the Imperial German Embassy, then one of the most splendid diplomatic mansions in London, that Holmes would almost certainly have gone to receive the order conferred upon him by 'the Hereditary King of Bohemia'. Though, *in theory,* the so-called 'independent member-states of the German Empire' —Baden, Mecklenburg-Strelitz, Bavaria, and so forth—were mere provinces of the German Empire. A glance at the Diplomatic List of 1892 shews that though Great Britain sent ministers to these 'independent' kingdoms and grandduchies, they sent none to London. The 'interests were guarded' by the Imperial German (ie, Prussian) Ambassador in London.

For those who, unlike Holmes, have never had an order conferred upon them, let me point out that the splendid appearance of a man glittering with orders is not achieved without some quite considerable monetary outlay. Except in the case of the highest grades of orders of chivalry—and those conferred on persons of outstanding merit or fame (and sometimes even of both)—or in the case of the lowest grades issued in wholesale quantities, all that the person honoured actually gets is a citation conferring the order upon him.

In many cases, as happened when my friend, the late Prince Melikoff, was awarded the Order of the Lion and Sun of Persia (with Diamond Sword of Honour), the star of the order is pinned on the chest, and the coruscating sword belted about the waist.

Then, with deep bows, the newly-honoured walks backwards to the portières, tall drapes held open by gorgeously-dressed flunkeys, and, once outside the throne chamber, the 'property' jewels are taken off, and a trade-card is handed to the new member of the order— with the name of a jeweller on it, who has a stock of such gauds.

That was in Teheran, fifty years ago. It is a little better today, though not much. Many countries do actually give the decoration itself, as well as the impressively written document of authorisation to wear it; but the decoration is in 'economy' metals, and if you wish for something a little more valuable, you buy it yourself. In any case, the moment one's name appears in the country's official gazette as having been selected for an honour, one will be sent full-colour catalogues of orders in every precious metal and adorned with every precious stone.

In Holmes's younger days, the situation almost everywhere was much as my friend's description of the conditions in Teheran in 1924. Anything worth wearing, even in London—perhaps *especially* in London—one bought oneself.

Fortunately, there were plenty of high-class jewellers, specialising in making up orders and decorations to customers' particular requirements; nor were they backward in bringing their services to the notice of a potential customer.

Fortunately, too, the new customer could choose any one of a number of firms offering their services, secure in the knowledge that their products had been endorsed by patrons of the utmost respectability. There was Lambert, Goldsmiths, Jewellers and Silversmiths to HM the Queen, HRH the Prince of Wales, the Duke of Edinburgh and many another notables. On the brick front of their old-fashioned shop at 10, 11 and 12 Coventry Street, the firm displayed the royal arms and the three feathers of the Prince of Wales. Lambert's old Georgian shop went when Lyons's Coventry Street Corner House was built in 1908, and Lambert's moved to New Bond Street where, happily, they continue to serve what remains of taste and wealth in our impoverished society. Holmes may well have asked Lambert's to supply his CB, CVO and CMG.

But, in a time and in a city so rich as London was in the 1890s, Lambert's had many rivals, all of them honoured with a royal warrant. There were J. W. Benson Ltd (HM the Queen, HRH the Prince of Wales), then in Ludgate Hill, but bombed out in World

Regent Street, taken from the opposite side of what is now Oxford Circus but was then called 'Regent Circus.' All of this scene has changed today save the tall domed building on the right and the gentlemen's subterranean retiring-room on the left. The pedestrians seem almost as divergently and as oddly dressed as they are today!

War II to move to New Bond Street. There were Carrington & Co, and R. S. Garrard & Co, both of Regent Street, still there and previously mentioned. Garrard's, then as now, were Crown Jewellers and Goldsmiths. Carrington's held warrants from the Queen and the Prince and Princess of Wales; Garrard's from the Queen and the Prince only.

Similar distinctions had been earned by Elkington & Co—their splendid showrooms at 22 Regent Street are now occupied by the Ceylon Tea Centre—and Hancocks & Co, then of 152 New Bond Street, but who have now been 'developed' out of Vigo Street, and have moved their fine stock to new premises at 1 Burlington Gardens, SW. R. & L. Kock, jewellers, of Frankfurt-on-Main, may have sent their catalogue to Holmes, not only in connection with his British but also his other decorations. Kock's supplied the Prince of Wales for his generous moods when in Germany, but they may have been a little too foreign, a little too smart, for Holmes. Another jeweller's establishment patronised by the Prince on his trips abroad was that of Emile Pardonneau, of 18 rue Royale, Paris. He almost certainly sent his catalogue to Holmes, but here again I think that Holmes's prejudice against the Prince cannot have permitted him seriously to entertain the thought of patronising Pardonneau. However, since the article in question was one that the French jeweller supplied often, Holmes may have ordered his Legion of Honour there. Perhaps.

More to Holmes's reserved tastes were probably A. Marx & Co, of 121 Regent Street, and Ortner & Houle, of 3 St James's Street, though the slightly more competitive prices, and the more 'go-ahead' character of Rowlands & Frazer, of 146 Regent Street (The Queen, the Prince and the Princess of Wales) may have appealed to Holmes.

An old-fashioned, 'good' firm at that time was F. B. Thomas & Co, of 153 New Bond Street; as also was Henry Tessier, then of 106 Mount Street, and now, and for many years, in New Bond Street.

Tiffany's of New York could make a living in London in those days, and magnificently rebuilt the New Bond Street premises just after the first World War with black marble columns with gilded Corinthian capitals flanking the wealth-breathing entrance. But alas! beating the Kaiser had put the British Empire in perpetual hock to the White House, and Tiffany's closed down their London branch. The magnificent shop-front still remains, but for many years now it has been a branch of Lotus, the shoe manufacturers.

With all these jewellers available, where did Holmes eventually go? Fortunately, as I have explained elsewhere*, there is a clue in the fact that Watson always used a name familiar to him rather than hunt around for a name picked at random out of a newspaper, directory, or suchlike.

Now, in the case of 'Wisteria Lodge', the most unusual name of 'Marx' appears. Not only that, but it occurs in the form, 'Marx & Co'. True, the 'Marx & Co' of 'Wisteria Lodge' make clothing, not the royally-bestowed ornaments to make clothing more glamorous. Still, there *is* a connection between 'clothing' and 'clothing oneself with orders and decorations', and what makes it more probable that Watson had this in mind when he chose the name, 'Marx & Co' for use in 'Wisteria Lodge' is that, of all the possible—indeed, of all the probable—names of jewellers to which Holmes went for his decorations, only that A. Marx & Co, of 121

In the Footsteps of Sherlock Holmes (revised edition), David & Charles, 1971.

Regent Street, W, is almost identical with that used for the clothing manufacturers mentioned in the case of 'Wisteria Lodge'.

A. Marx & Co have left 121 Regent Street these many years. The expiration of the 99-years Crown leases between 1913 and 1923 drove many of the smaller firms from Regent Street, since to stay in their premises there entailed rebuilding on the strength of only a further 99-years lease. Some well-known firms tried to meet the conditions imposed by the Commissioners of Crown Lands—*not* the Crown itself, republicans please note?—but, after sinking hundreds of thousands of pounds in the erection of new premises, found themselves short of working capital and had to drop out of the unequal struggle. Amongst such was the internationally famous Isobel, but many other famous Regent Street shops went the same way: the Cricklite Lamp & Light Co (No 132), Pope & Plante, Hosiers, Glovers and Shirt Makers, of 136 Regent Street ('Surgical elastic stockings and kneecaps, for varicose veins and weakness'), J. C. Vickery, the famous jewellers and travelling-bag manufacturers, of 181 & 193 Regent Street.

Other vanishings, after often quite lengthy battles against inevitable extinction, included that most famous shop with Victorian families, H. J. Nicoll & Co, which contrived to keep going in its new, expensive premises until World War II. Its imposing frontage on Regent Street now houses a branch of Montague Burton 'the Tailor of Taste'. Other casualties were the big drapery store of Howell & James Ltd (HM the Queen, HRH the Prince and Princess of Wales), 5, 7, & 9, Regent Street, Gérard et Cie, florists, 178 Regent Street, Jules Duvelleroy, fan manufacturer, 167 Regent Street (moved to New Bond Street), Elkington & Co, 22 Regent Street (they didn't have to rebuild, but they failed to stay the course, all the same), Alexander Jones & Co, dressing-case manufacturers and stationers, 154 Regent Street, John Lobb, bootmaker, 296 Regent Street (moved to St James's Street), Roberts & Co, billiard-table manufacturers, 99 Regent Street, Schott & Co, music-sellers, 157 & 159 Regent Street (they held a warrant from HM the Queen, herself so dedicated a lover of music that she was taking lessons 'in the piano-forte' only six years before her death in 1901), Tiffany & Co, of 221 & 221a—note the number!—Regent Street (they moved, as we have seen, to New Bond Street), Waléry Ltd, photographers, 164 Regent Street (they photographed the

Queen in her old age) and John Walker, watchmaker, of 230 Regent Street. These are some of the royal warrant-holding casualties of Regent Street's rebuilding in the period just after World War I.

Now there is an important point to notice here: the number of Tiffany's, the jewellers in Regent Street, at the time when Holmes (accompanied, surely, by Watson) was ordering 'better class' versions of the orders and decorations which had been conferred upon him by the many royalties and governments considered above.

In a short paper contributed to *The Baker Street Journal**, I discussed a theory of mine which sought to explain why Watson had chosen the (admittedly imaginary) number '221B Baker Street' which, in the rough note reproduced on page 43, was intended to be '221B *Upper* Baker Street'. Without precisely abandoning the theory examined in that article, I must call attention to the fact that a search for an imaginary number for their apartments in Baker Street might well have been ended for Watson when, picking up a bill from Tiffany's, he noticed the numbers of their premises in Regent Street, and muttered: '221 . . . 221a . . .' and added idly: '. . . 221B!'

Was *this* the origin of that famous, mysterious and still widely and hotly debated number? If so, it does surely follow that Tiffany bills were arriving in Baker Street—in those days, no one paid cash— though whether for 'custom built' orders and decorations or merely for the cigarette- and cigar-cases which are mentioned or implied by the many references to smoking in the Canon, it is not possible yet to say.

But the, possibly coincidental, nearness of Tiffany's real number in Regent Street to the (known to be of Watson's fabrication, and so imaginary) number of the Holmes-Watson apartments in Baker Street does admit the possibility that Tiffany's as well as A. Marx & Co were known to Watson, since he used the former's number and the latter's name in the Canon.

Perhaps future research will positively identify the firm or firms of jewellers who 'had the honour' of making up orders and decorations 'to the esteemed instructions of Mr Sherlock Holmes'. In any case, Watson himself was entitled to at least two campaign medals as the result of his Indian and Afghan experiences, and these he may

---

*'Why 221B?' *The Baker Street Journal*, An Irregular Journal of Sherlockiana (Julian Wolff, MD, Editor), Vol 14, No 4, p 219; New Series, December 1964.

well have ordered from Tiffany's (or Marx's). Perhaps Holmes patronised either or both of these well-known jewellers because they were already known to Watson?

CHAPTER 8

The Changing Face of Scotland Yard

If a visitor to London today were to ask a policeman, 'Will you please direct me to Scotland Yard?' the policeman, if he be of the old-fashioned, obliging type, will ask 'Great Scotland Yard or New Scotland Yard?', and no doubt go on to explain that Great Scotland Yard is a narrow street connecting Whitehall with Northumberland Avenue, whereas New Scotland Yard is a flat-faced, featureless building in Victoria Street, at the corner of Broadway. It is only a few years old but, beginning with the usual modern architectural handicaps, it is a building of the sort which does not improve with age. It is the third 'New Scotland Yard' to date, and cannot possibly be the last: Parkinson's Law operates just as effectively in police, as in any other bureaucracy.

Holmes knew two of what, for brevity, are popularly called 'Scotland Yards'—the old Metropolitan Police Office in Whitehall Gardens (just off the street named Great Scotland Yard; now best known for the Army Recruiting Office situated there), and New Scotland Yard, the red-brick and stone baronial fortress lying between Whitehall and the Embankment, just a little to the west of Richmond Terrace. This new headquarters for the Metropolitan Police was opened, so far as the Derby Street, Whitehall, part was concerned, in 1891, the frontage on the Embankment being added in 1912.

An extension to New Scotland Yard was added in 1938, so it is possible that Holmes knew this, too. It is a very plain eight-storey building faced with Portland stone, and has its main entrance on

Victoria Embankment. In design, it was intended to merge with the multiple-block government office eventually planned to extend from Whitehall Gardens to Bridge Street, of which most of the portion from Whitehall Gardens to Richmond Terrace has now been erected.

London's police system actually began, not in Whitehall, but in the Bow Street magistrates' court where, under the novelist and enlightened jurist, Henry Fielding, who became a London stipendiary magistrate in 1748, the foundations of a detective police force —the renowned 'Bow Street Runners'—were laid.

After Fielding's death, his work was carried on, even more efficiently, by his blind half-brother, Sir John, under whom the Bow Street Runners achieved both maximum expertise and maximum fame. They really did begin to track down criminals, and *prove* criminal intent and action; and, despite the fact that their glory was somewhat sullied by their having been headed by the notorious Jonathan Wild, their success was such as to induce the younger Pitt, in 1785, to introduce his police bill, though it was not until 1829 that, under Sir Robert Peel, the Metropolitan Police force, as we know it today, was eventually organised.

A separate detective police force, consisting of an inspector and six constables, all 'plain clothesmen', was organised in 1843; and though this is not generally conceded, I think it is plain that this force owed much, if not all of its origin to the success of the Post Office laboratory, set up in Bell Yard, Fleet Street (just by Temple Bar), to conduct a *scientific* war against those essentially postal offences that the introduction of pre-paid Penny Post (6 May 1840) had made possible and profitable. This Post Office crime laboratory still exists, and its story is one of not-often-interrupted success; though its work in intercepting the mail of Italian revolutionaries, with their consequent denunciation to the Austrian authorities, raised a storm of protest in Parliament.

Following Pitt's action to endorse the long, patient work of the Fielding brothers, nine police-offices were operating in London by 1800; revolutionary activities in France and a flood of refugees from that country having presented the Government with problems which emphasised the necessity of an efficient police force.

Until the organisation of the Metropolitan Police under the then Home Secretary, Sir Robert Peel, the headquarters of London's

As Home Secretary, 1828, Sir Robert Peel was chiefly responsible for giving Britain a modern police force, whose members were popularly known as 'Peelers' or 'Bobbies'. Here is a typical 'Peeler', with top hat, 'bulls-eye' lantern and rattle. The rattle was soon exchanged for the truncheon, but the top hat remained regulation wear until 1864, when it was replaced by the ancestor of the present 'Roman' helmet police administration remained where it had begun in the mid-eighteenth century: at Bow Street, still the court of the chief metropolitan magistrate, and the court where most of London's more important criminal cases have their preliminary hearing.

Moving the headquarters of the Metropolitan Police to Great Scotland Yard after the Peel reforms of 1829 involved re-housing the new police in some still not-too-old eighteenth-century buildings, but by 1850 the original police buildings had grown unsuitable. The premises were then rebuilt, the Metropolitan Police occupying one separate building, and the Public Carriage Office another separate, but smaller, building.

These plain yellow-brick and stone buildings were amongst the many objects of attack in the nearly thirty-year reign of terror conducted by the Dynamiters against (mostly London) targets: bridges, trains, private houses, clubs, stations, monuments (sixteen cakes of dynamite, already fused, were removed from Nelson's Column before they could be detonated). At 9.20 pm, on 30 May 1884, a bomb nearly wrecked the detective department in Great Scotland Yard and completely demolished a nearby pub, as full it seems of off-duty police as of members of the public. Many were injured, two very seriously.

Six years later, all departments of the Metropolitan Police were moved to their new home off Derby Street, at the Whitehall corner of which is the (rebuilt 1895) old pub, 'The Red Lion', mentioned in *David Copperfield*.

A glance at Holmes's cases for the period January 1884-August 1886 reveals the curious, and doubtless fortunate, fact that none of these, from 'The Delicate Case of the King of Scandinavia' to 'The Little Problem of the Grosvenor Square Furniture Van', would have necessitated Holmes's calling at Great Scotland Yard. He was thus never in any danger from unworthy attempts to bomb the very focus of London's law and order.

In 1891, when Lestrade and Company went down the road from Great Scotland Yard to New Scotland Yard, Holmes was almost certainly not in England: he was engaged, you may recall, in 'The Matter of Supreme Importance to the French Government' (which was also having its troubles with disaffected bomb-throwers). And by Monday, 4 May 1891, Holmes, after having appeared to fall into the Reichenbach Falls after Moriarty, thought it prudent to stay out of sight until the time came to reveal himself to Watson on Thursday, 5 April 1894—just in time, a cynic might observe, to help Watson with his income-tax figures for the year 1893-4.

So that, by the time Inspector Stanley Hopkins had been helped in four cases by Holmes (between early December 1896 and late January 1897), the Scotland Yard men had had opportunity to settle down in their new headquarters.

These new police headquarters had a curious origin, the evidence of which is still to be seen in the basement. The Victoria Embankment, replacing mud flats on which jetties, groynes, boats, barges and a floating police office made an artistic confusion, was built between 1864 and 1870. Noble buildings were to line it, and amongst the first to be proposed was a National Theatre, or, to be more precise, a National Opera House.

The work was undertaken with enthusiasm, and to this date no satisfactory reason has been advanced for the failure to complete the building. The architect, Francis H. Fowler, had prepared the plans for the Opera House, which was to have been one-third larger than Covent Garden, and the foundation stone was laid by the Duke of Edinburgh (later Reigning Duke of Saxe-Coburg and Gotha), Queen Victoria's sailor son, on 16 December 1875, it being intended that the building should be completed by the end of 1877. Foundations were laid and the basement dressing-rooms and other parts completed. And then work stopped—through lack of funds, it was said, but this does not seem to be the real reason. Was it that royal interest was transferred to the Albert Hall? Hardly, since that building, suggested by the Prince Consort and carried through after his death by General Scott, had been completed in 1871, four years before the Duke of Edinburgh laid the foundation stone of the National Opera House. It is a most mysterious business.

Nothing more was done after the building had risen from sub-basement to ground level, and the uncompleted building remained, one of London's more notable eyesores, until, the site having remained derelict for fifteen years, it was turned over to the Metropolitan Police, who were looking for important land on which to build a new headquarters. Norman Shaw, one of the most intelligent and imaginative architects of the post-Classical school, was commissioned to prepare designs. The present 'ex-New Scotland Yard' —threatened with 'development' as 'redundant' on the transfer of the various Metropolitan Police departments to the 'New New Scotland Yard' in Victoria Street but now (as I write) the subject of second thoughts—was the result of Shaw's architectural planning. He was restricted, of course, by the fact that he ha ' to incorporate an already existing, and extensive, basement building into his plans; that he succeeded so well despite this important restriction, shows the quality of his talent.

Perhaps Shaw's best-known work was the new Gaiety Theatre at the corner of the Strand and the western tip of Aldwych, which opened with *The Orchid* (transferred from the old Gaiety Theatre) on 26 October 1903. The death of this theatre after the second World War is a mystery on which, I think, the last word has by no means been said. It was one of the handsomest buildings ever to embellish a capital not noticeably rich in beautiful buildings, and its successor—an office building erected as a speculation by the Indian Government, which bought the site of the demolished Gaiety —cannot compare in looks with the Shaw masterpiece it displaced. Two ugly and meaningless 'symbolic' statues surmount the canopy of the front entrance and, like so many other 'symbolic' statues, are now completely inapposite since they were designed to 'adorn' a building leased by the Electricity Council, which has now found other premises. The building is now occupied by the City National Bank of New York.

New Scotland Yard—that 'Yard' which became familiar to Holmes after his return to London in 1894—was many things: an administrative headquarters, a laboratory, an office for licensing hackney carriages (and, after 1897, mechanically-driven vehicles, which are denominated, in the quaint phraseology of The Yard, as 'mechanical clarences'), a central records office, and a 'black museum'. But it was never, in the widest use of the phrase, a 'police station'. The police station that most people think of as part of The Yard is Cannon Row police station, which is in a narrow street leading from Derby Street to Bridge Street, and running parallel with Whitehall.

More people know the big pub at the corner, the 'St Stephen's Tavern' (a favourite with the plainclothes men from Cannon Row and The Yard) than they do the dingy police station in the narrow street on to which the pub's side-entrance gives. It is an old-fashioned as well as a dingy police station, but it has an outstanding

Detectives, private and police, in 1887—according to the illus-
trator of ' A Study in Scarlet's ' first edition, 1887
(*Left to right*) Dr Watson (in curly topper and curly mous-
tache), Holmes (in inverness, but with a billycock hat), and the
two ' Yard ' detectives, Lestrade and Gregson, the latter looking
like a railway guard flagging down a runaway train

importance in the history of British crime, since many a notable criminal has been brought here to be charged before being taken next door, to The Yard, to be interrogated, or vice versa.

Amongst the many duties of the Metropolitan Police is that of supervising 'common lodging houses', far more of which existed in the last century than today. In 1881, when Holmes took up residence with Watson in Baker Street, the officer attached to 'A' Division responsible for inspection of common lodging-houses was Inspector Thomas Holmes, which may or may not have some bearing on the readiness of Lestrade and other CID men to pick Holmes's brains —'Lestrade is a well-known detective. He got himself into a fog recently over a forgery case, and that was what brought him here'.

It is possible, too, that Holmes may have had other, family, connections with the Force. My researches into the contemporary police background to Holmes's earliest detective activities revealed two possibly significant facts: that in 1881, the year of Holmes's first really important case, 'A Study in Scarlet', 'B' Division of the Metropolitan Police was under the charge of Chief Inspector James *Sherlock*, whilst 'L' Division (Lambeth, where Enoch J. Drebber had died at 3 Lauriston Gardens, Brixton Road) was under the charge of Chief Inspector William *Sherlock*.*

On the other hand, it has been remarked that at no time could Holmes's relationship with The Yard have been described as cordial. Always willing to help the police, Holmes yet makes no attempt to conceal his contempt for the individual police officer, detective or otherwise, or, generally, for the institution they repre-sent. He accuses them of using him to gain their ends, and then of denying him the credit for solutions they are either too lazy or too brainless to provide. Left to himself, Holmes usually manages to effect 'justice' in a manner not at all within the Law. 'It is every man's business to see justice done', he says, rather unctuously, in 'The Adventure of Shoscombe Old Place', but we know he intends us to understand that it is *his* conception of justice he wishes to pursue. It occurs to me that there may be a hint of the cause of this enduring enmity between Holmes and the police in the first few pages of 'A Study in Scarlet'.

If you remember how Watson and Holmes met at Bart's Hospital through the introduction of 'young Stamford', you will also recall

---

*See 'A Study in Surmise', *Ellery Queen's Mystery Magazine,* February 1971.

that, before Stamford had a chance to utter the immortal 'Dr Watson, Mr Sherlock Holmes'—commemorated on the bronze plaque in the 'Path. Lab.'—this had happened: —

> At the sound of our steps he glanced round and sprang to his feet with a cry of pleasure. 'I've found it! I've found it', he shouted to my companion, running towards him with a test-tube in his hand, 'I have found a re-agent which is precipitated by haemoglobin, and by nothing else.' . . .

and to Watson and 'young Stamford' Holmes explains:—

> 'Why, man, it is the most practical medico-legal discovery for years. Don't you see that it gives us an infallible test for blood stains.'

And its value . . . ?

> '. . . Had this test been invented, there are hundreds of men now walking the earth who would long ago have paid the penalty of their crimes.'
>
> 'Indeed, I murmured.'

Others, too, must have murmured 'Indeed!' when Holmes, full of enthusiasm, sought to put his 'infallible' test at the disposal of Authority. For that Holmes was snubbed is certain, and not only by the British police. The first important case to prove the ability of forensic scientists to detect human bloodstains was that of Lucie Berlin's murder, in Berlin, in 1904; and not until several years after this did British detectives begin to employ similar tests.

Now all this slow progress towards the detection of human blood, and towards the ability to distinguish it, not only from animal blood but from human blood of other 'groups', was based on the researches of von Behring in the 1890s (ten years and more after Holmes's discovery) and, notably, those of Uhlenluth who, in 1900, published his serum test.

Holmes's discovery was, one assumes, never acted upon: another example, doubtless, of that strange inverse xenophobia of British Authority, which will accept new ideas only when they seem to have a foreign origin. But, in the face of such a snub—and remember that Holmes, in 1881, was only twenty-seven, with all a young man's hot reaction to unjustified contempt—it is no wonder that Holmes, nursing an unconquerable prejudice against the British police system, preferred to go his own highly individual way.

CHAPTER 9

On Dress and Other Matters

So long, [wrote the author of *The Glass of Fashion* (1881)] as the present constitution of Society endures, Dress must always remain a matter of some importance; and rightly so, for it is a duty we owe to others as well as to ourselves to make the best of our personal appearance . . . After all, a man's dress is still, to some extent, an index to his character. Study his hat, his coat, the fit of his trousers, the shape of his boots, and you will arrive at some notion of his taste and judgment . . . It is often asserted that nowadays all classes dress alike; the clerk like the peer, the wife of a London tradesman like the wife of a blue-blooded patrician. Is it so? The various articles of which their attire is made up—its component parts, so to speak—may be the same, but they differ in that indefinable something which is the impress made on a person's dress by a person's character. You can tell the gentleman from the snob, however they may be dressed; they *wear* their clothes differently'.

'The present constitution of Society' of which the author wrote was to endure, almost unchanged, until the outbreak of World War I, a matter of some thirty-five years; and, quite importantly changed, but still enduring, until about 1960. After that the principles of the new anarchical society became dominant, and dress ceased to be a matter of importance to the élite of the Hand-Out Culture.

It must not be thought that cast-off army uniforms have never before been worn by down-and-out civilians; they have, and it was because of this abuse of 'the Queen's uniform' that the Uniforms Act of 1894, making it a punishable offence for a civilian to wear a Service uniform, in part or in total, or any dress designed to imitate any Service uniform (the Act also covered the unauthorised wearing of medals, orders and rank-badges), was passed. What provided the impetus to the energy manifested by the framers of the Bill was the enterprise of a sandwich-men's 'jobmaster', who dressed up his scarecrow squad in old army uniforms, and paraded these wretched drop-outs in a parody, at once ludicrous and pathetic, of Service discipline. The Act—which is now treated by the police as a dead-letter (apparently on their own authority)—stopped this use of cast-off military and naval uniforms until what Macmillan called 'the wind of change' made their wearing both possible and fashionable.

The late Sidney Paget, with his incomparable opportunities of recording the main items of Mr Sherlock Holmes's obviously extensive wardrobe, has shewn us Holmes in a number of greatly contrasting costumes—the significance of the contrast having, one regrets to note, quite escaped the clothes-unconscious play–and film-makers of to-day.

No matter what the present opinion on 'suitable dress' is, no one in Holmes's day would wear—as he is made to wear in film after film—a double-peaked travelling cap and long tweed Inverness for, say, a stroll along Baker Street or a call at a Belgrave Square mansion. No one who could afford it in pre-1914 days would ever wear an *unsuitable* costume, and the well-dressed man and woman would feel obliged to change several times a day in order to maintain the 'suitability' of their dress. (The idea survives in our still current phrase, 'morning dress'.)

Holmes and Watson, like all other men of their day, were allowed considerable licence in the matter of their dress's *details* —as is evident from Paget's drawings of Holmes and Watson, separately or together—but a journey to the country necessitated *country* dress; a walk through Regent Street would not have been made in a tweed suit; a call on a 'respectable' person would have been made in frock-coat and (usually) topper, though Paget records one of Holmes's graver eccentricities in showing him in morning-coat and a *bowler*—a dismal solecism perpetrated by the late

Benito Mussolini, the late King Amanullah of Afghanistan, and Dr Crippen, the wife-slayer.

Though a point to remember here is that Holmes's dress-sense evidently improved with his expanding and ameliorating practice, and, as a consequence, with his increasing income. The small fees he was earning in 1880 and 1881—the cases of the Tarleton Murders, of Vamberry the Wine Merchant, of the Old Russian Woman, of the Trifling Affair of Mortimer Maberley—had given place, over the years of growing prestige, to the lordly sums extracted from kings and peers and prime ministers. Would even Holmes have thought, in 1881, of being able to charge what he charged the Duke of Holdernesse*, in 1901: £6,000? One feels that, two years later, when called in by the Sultan of Turkey, Holmes asked an even higher fee, if only to avoid the risk of being despised by the Sultan as a cheap-skate.

Obviously, Holmes's ability to patronise better tailors, hatters, bootmakers and other essential tradesmen depended, as it must with us all, on the state of his purse. Holmes, it is clear from Watson's narratives, 'never looked back' as they say: there are no reckless and unfortunate investments in a period of shady fortunes made at the expense of mugs. Wherever Holmes invested his money, it wasn't in empty Australian and South African gold mines, in catchpenny building societies or insurance companies, such as were then enriching their discoverers or founders, and impoverishing thousands of investors chasing the fast buck.

Perhaps, at the beginning of his career, when he could not afford to take the apartments in Baker Street unless he could find someone to share the small rent with him, Holmes might have patronised such a tailor as Charles Baker & Co, of Tottenham Court Road, a twenty-minute walk along Marylebone Road, past Madame Tussaud's, from Baker Street. Charles Baker & Co would make a 'sound' suit, to measure, from as little as twenty-five shillings; 'superior quality' from thirty shillings.

As things improved, as they did rather quickly with Holmes—he had Mrs Farintosh, owner of the opal tiara, as a client within a few months of settling down in Baker Street with Watson—he could

---

*So His Grace is called in 'The Adventure of the Priory School', but in 'The Adventure of the Blanched Soldier', Holmes reveals that he was really the Duke of Greyminster.

have afforded to pay a little more for his clothes, and in that dress-conscious London there were even more tailors than there are pillar-boxes to-day.

W. Shingleton, of 60 New Bond Street, was a well-known tailor in what was then a more fashionable street than it is now. Yet all that Shingleton charged for a morning suit (what the Americans call a 'Prince Albert') was four guineas; a frock-suit or dress-suit, both silk-faced and silk-lined, cost from five guineas upwards; but one could get an ulster at Shingleton's for as little as two guineas—all these clothes, of course, made to one's measure.

We know that, as his fame grew and his bank-balance with it, Holmes became increasingly dress-conscious; even, one has to admit, to the point of censoriousness in the matter of others' sartorial insufficiencies.

That almost finicky attention to dress he had permitted himself to develop by the middle of 1889 (only eight years after joining up with Watson), is shown by Holmes's attitude towards an eminent peer's economising in the matter of boots, a good, hand-made-to-measure pair of which could be bought in 1889 for a guinea.

> 'We are now going to interview Lord Holdhurst, the Cabinet Minister and future Premier of England,' Holmes tells Watson; and when the interview is over: 'He's a fine fellow', said Holmes, as we came out into Whitehall. But he has a struggle to keep up his position. He is far from rich, and has many calls. You noticed, of course, *that his boots had been resoled?* [My italics: M.H.]

If Holmes was as intolerant of sloppy dressing by May-June 1889, one may imagine how particular, in matter of dress, he had become by mid-1901 when, at the request of Dr Thorneycroft Huxtable, MA, PhD etc, he called on the Duke of Holdernesse (or Greyminster) in the matter of the Duke's missing heir, Lord Saltire.

By then, Holmes would certainly have taken his custom to *the* London tailor, with royal warrants from both HM the Queen and the Prince of Wales: Henry Poole & Co, 'Civil, Court, Diplomatic and Military Tailors', of 36-39 Savile Row. (One sent one's servants to their livery department, tactfully situated several streets away at 21 Clifford Street.)

Poole's had an unusual reputation, in one respect not unlike that of the Yorkshire dressmaker, Worth, who had taken Paris by storm; though Poole's were tailors, not dress-makers. Both these eminent firms dressed the cream of the *demi-monde* as well as the cream of the *monde*. Poole had made the *paletot* that Skittles (Catherine Walters), one of the most notorious and rapacious strumpets of the 1860s, had made famous; but, as I have pointed out, both the Queen and her clothes-conscious heir were happy to let Poole cut their habits and suits for them.

In, say 1900, Poole charged twenty guineas for a dress-coat, and from about twelve guineas for a 'short jacket' suit, in which Paget has portrayed Holmes.

However, there were other tailors patronised by the Prince of Wales, and all within easy reach of Baker Street: Davies & Son, 19 & 20 Hanover Street, Hanover Square; Thomas Davis & Co, 12 Regent Street; Thomas Doughty, 1 Brook Street; Grant & Cockburn (famous for their leather breeches), 23 Piccadilly; H. Huntsman & Sons (famous for their riding habits, especially breeches, and still tailors to the British royal family), 41 Albemarle Street; Meyer & Mortimer, Army Tailors, 36 Conduit Street; Newton & Bean, 7 Hanover Square; Price, Whittaker & Co, 6 Suffolk Street; Skinner & Co, 57 Jermyn Street. And of course, equally fashionable tailors, such as the much-patronised A. Atkinson ('Speciality —Dress Suits'), of 33 Brook Street, Grosvenor Square, who, for some reason or other, had not secured 'the honour of supplying a royal household'.

I think we can say with some confidence that, out of the list of tailors just given one at least enjoyed the patronage of the Baker Street household; if of both Watson *and* Holmes, then almost certainly through Watson's introduction. This is the firm of Meyer & Mortimer, and I base my guess on Watson's well-known habit of choosing to hide real names under names which were familiar to him.

You will recall that the adventure of *The Hound of the Baskervilles* begins with the appearance of 'Dr James Mortimer', formerly of Charing Cross Hospital, much of whose original fabric (the foundation-stones were laid by the Duke of Richmond & Gordon in 1828 and by the Duke of Sussex in 1830) still exists. Watson also bestows the pseudonym of 'Mortimer' on a gardener in the case of 'The Golden Pince-Nez': the name 'Mortimer' was evidently familiar to Watson, and I suggest it was because it was the name of his regimental tailor. And, to clinch the argument, the name 'Adolph Meyer' occurs again in 'The Bruce-Partington Plans'.

Clothes are mentioned frequently in the Canon. From Watson we learn that Holmes's wardrobe contained at least: —

> a long grey cloak
> an overcoat (mentioned five times)
> an ulster (possibly the same overcoat)
> a tweed suit
> a dress suit
> flannels and blazer (since Watson mentions tennis shoes)
> frock suit (since Watson mentions a silk hat)
> 3 dressing-gowns—dull grey, mouse-coloured and purple (mentioned no fewer than eighteen times!)

In addition, we have the pictorial testimony of Sidney Paget that he had a tweed travelling cap (the now famous 'deer-stalker'), a bowler, a homburg, a soft felt, and a morning suit (a 'Prince Albert'). Though Sidney Paget does not shew Holmes in anything but a turndown ('come to Jesus') collar, Watson's mention of a cravat points clearly to the use, on occasions, of a 'wing' collar. Watson makes the remark, in 'The Musgrave Ritual', that Holmes was a 'prim' dresser; taken in conjunction with his criticism of Lord Holdhurst's boots, one could fairly say that Holmes was a man more than ordinarily careful of his clothes. His wardrobe would have contained at least one set of clothes proper to all normal occasions. And that, of course, included his Court dress. He would have had, too, a dress overcoat, with silk-faced lapels, to wear over tails or smoking jacket (the term 'dinner jacket' did not come in until about 1912).

The indispensable accessories to elegant dressing Watson does not mention—the mention of the cravat in 'A Study in Scarlet' is exceptional—but there was no shortage of shops at which they might be bought. Prices for shirts were low: even as late as 1900 when, owing to the (so far disastrous) Boer War, prices, stable for twenty years, were beginning to rise, W. Drake, Shirt & Collar Maker, 43 New Bridge Street, EC, was advertising his 'Perfect Shirt' in twelve styles, in superior longcloth or fine Irish linen four-fold, at 4s 6d each or 26s for six, carriage paid. Other items of apparel were no dearer: excellent (starched) linen collars could be bought for 3s a dozen, and the very finest quality was never more than 6d a collar.

Watson mentions, as I have said, Holmes's dressing-gowns and one must assume pyjamas, rather than a nightshirt, underneath. For even though Sherlock, as was noticed earlier, might have been a bit 'old-fashioned', a bit 'set in his ways', Watson's Indian and Afghan experiences would have introduced him to, and given him a liking for, pyjamas; Sherlock must have adopted them, too, 'advanced' though this type of sleeping-suit (the original name was 'pyjama sleeping-suit') must have seemed to Holmes. Sampson & Co, of 129-130 Oxford Street ('opposite Harewood Gate', the advertisements said) offered 'pyjama sleeping-suits at 12s 6d, 16s 6d, and 25s' in one of the earliest trade-mentions that I have been able to trace—a curious comment on prices, for I bought some excellent pyjamas, in 1939, at Austin Reed's for 10s 6d a pair. Sampson's, by the way,—their shop was within walking distance of Baker Street, a penny on the Atlas bus—advertised 'surplice' shirts at 45s and 57s a dozen or 3s 9d and 4s 9d each, respectively.

Hats were what even the Victorians called cheap, prices having stabilised about mid-century into what might be called 'traditional cost'. Competition did not begin to erode standard prices until the latter part of the century, when Dunn, of Whitechapel High Street, founder of the now famous and nationwide Dunn & Co, Hatters (they now sell clothes as well), produced his 'three-and-ninepenny' hat, soft or hard felt, and began to make a dent in the 'standardised' price list. You will recall that, at the Mad Hatter's Tea Party, the Hatter himself has a label, 'In this Style, 10s 6d', stuck in the hat-band.

Half-a-guinea for a tall hat—the 'topper' as the British call it—became standard price about 1830 and remained so for nearly a century. However, from the look of some of the hats that Sherlock wore, one suspects that his parsimonious nature inclined him to encourage the price-cutting Dunn.

The sartorial element—often, indeed, the sartorial factor—occurs frequently in the Canon: Sir Henry Baskerville's boots play an essential part in the mystery of his family's notorious spectral hound.

Sir Henry must have paid a little over the standard price for the boots he had bought in the Strand; it was, you may recall, 26s. In my book *In the Footsteps of Sherlock Holmes**, I identified

---

* Revised edition, with entirely new illustrations, David & Charles, 1971.

the shop at which Sir Henry had bought a pair of brown boots in 1888 as that of G. H. Harris, at 418 Strand. Walter House, the property of the Corps of Commissionaires, whose headquarters is in Exchange Court, at the back, was built in 1907 on the site of Harris's old shop and other seventeenth-century property.

Harris's was opposite the old Tivoli Music Hall which, pulled down in 1914, was replaced eight years later by the Tivoli Cinema, now demolished to make way for a block of shops and offices. The Harris boot and shoe business, founded by the Harris brothers in 1865, moved in 1907 to the then new 'Simpson-in-the-Strand' buildings, where they flourished for many years. Alas, only a short while after I had interviewed them in their 'new' home about Sir Henry's boots, this old-established firm went out of business, a casualty in the ever-more-savage competition of modern commerce.

The identification of Sir Henry's boot-shop with Harris's at 418 Strand was made more than probable by the fact that theirs was the nearest shop for a man whose boots had just been stolen from his

The National Gallery in the days of the hansom and, except for the traffic, not changed since. At the north side of Trafalgar Square, it faces Northumberland Avenue, off which, in a narrow street, lay 'The Northumberland Hotel' where Sir Henry Baskerville stayed

hotel. He had registered at the 'Northumberland Arms', which Watson, perhaps shocked that a baronet (even one from Canada) could have stopped at a mere tavern, calls 'the Northumberland Hotel'. It stood, and still stands—its name now altered to 'The Sherlock Holmes'—at the corner of narrow Northumberland Street, Strand, and even narrower Craven Passage, a delightful survival in which two pubs and some small shops make a street leading to the ringing cavernousness of the arches beneath Charing Cross Station.

Upstairs in 'The Sherlock Holmes', where I have taken many a dedicated Sherlockian (mostly from abroad) to an excellent luncheon or dinner, there is the 'reproduction of the sitting-room at

'The Northumberland Arms' (Watson calls it 'The Northumberland Hotel') as it is today, renamed 'The Sherlock Holmes': a tavern and restaurant that the owners, Whitbread & Co Ltd, have converted into a museum of Sherlockiana

The reconstructed sitting-room at 221B Baker Street, as it is to be seen upstairs in ' The Sherlock Holmes '. First devised as part of the Festival of Britain Exhibition in 1951, the reconstruction, after having been on view to the public in an office in Baker Street, was moved to ' The Sherlock Holmes ' as a permanent feature of the tavern-restaurant in 1957

221B' created for the Exhibition year of 1951, and sited, in that year, at the offices of the Abbey (now Abbey-National) Building Society, at 220-224 Baker Street (which was once *Upper* Baker Street).

The room, sealed off from the public behind a wall of plate-glass, must be recognised as a masterly effort in pastiche, but did the Two Friends *really* live in such shabby comfort (and perhaps not even comfort) at 221B, Baker Street?

The real trouble in painting a portrait of 'Life with Sherlock', as I have pointed out elsewhere, is that despite Vincent Starrett's theory of Sherlockian time 'frozen' at an eternal 1895, the *professional* life of Holmes covered over *forty years*, a long period indeed, and one in which fashions, prices, points-of-view, ages, economic situations, governments, rulers and everything else changeable, changed. Lads who were at school when Sherlock moved into Montague Street in 1878 were about to retire when Sherlock nailed the treacherous von Bork in 1914. One is too apt to forget that the man who was just twenty-four when he moved into Montague Street was just sixty when, his country in danger, he came out of retirement to foil the plotters of Imperial Germany.

For one thing, he would not have worn a deer-stalker, though he would have continued to wear an ulster in 1914, especially when driving his car. What was it, by the way? A Rolls-Royce 'Silver Ghost'? A growling 96 hp Lorraine-Dietrich? A 41.9 hp Daimler, such as Sir Duncan Hay drove himself in the President's Cup race at Brooklands, on Monday, 8 June 1908? Or the tremendous 89.5 hp Fiat that Nazzarro raced for Mr D'Arcy Baker on the same day in the match for £500 between Mr S. F. Edge, as challenger, and Mr D'Arcy Baker? Or something much smaller, such as the 8.9 hp Sizaire that Col T. Cowper-Essex entered and raced in the President's Cup? Or, say, a 24.8 hp Mercedes or, to patronise home-products, a 21.4 hp Calthorpe?

Whatever the make of the car in which Holmes and Watson drove down, it was Watson's car that day, and I think (now that we have done with speculation about Holmes's choice of car) it would have been a modestly-powered, medium-priced job, say a 22.4 hp De La Buire, and both men would have worn 'motoring caps' with the talc-lensed goggles that the dusty roads of those days rendered essential to vision.

Certainly, deer-stalkers would not have been worn; at some time between, say 1895 and 1905, this type of hat had been barred from wear save *in* the country—not, as hitherto, including travel *to* and *from* the country. It was no longer regarded as permissable 'railway' headgear, and it had been barred from wear by motorists for purely practical reasons: its stiff peak got in the way of the essential motoring goggles, and, with a peak fore and aft (a distinction that it shared with the contemporary postman's helmet), the deer-stalker could not be reversed, as motorists were fond of reversing the peaked cap, so as to accommodate the goggles.

So we come back to the homely shabbiness of that reconstructed sitting-room, which seems to me far more *static*, in a temporal sense, than I think it must have been. Furniture was exceedingly cheap in the 1880s. Oetzmann & Co, whose advertisements the Editor of *The Baker Street Journal* likes to reproduce nostalgically on the back cover of his excellent publication, could supply all the furniture for a bedroom—bed, mattress, sheets, pillows, rug, ward-

Was this the advertisement which influenced Holmes's choice of car? And if so, which did he choose: the 18/24 hp phaeton, the 25/30 hp landaulet or the elegant 'Longbridge' 25/30 hp limousine, to seat seven?

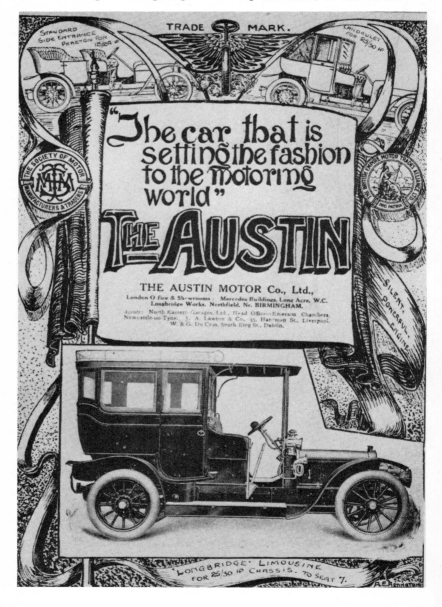

robe, wash-hand-stand, chest-of-drawers, towel-horse, bedside cabinet with carafe and tumbler on top and *vase de nuit* within, in decorated china—for five guineas, and furnishings for the other rooms in apartment or house were at the same highly competitive prices. One advertisement reproduced shows two 'drawing room' items from Oetzmann's stock. By chance we have the little occasional table (15s 9d in 1885): after nearly ninety years it is as sturdy as on the day it was bought.

No, I feel that the sitting-room, *as reproduced,* represents the Friends' focus-of-living as it may well have been at one short period of their shared existence; but that, as Holmes advanced in his profession and Watson, illness overcome, regained his, success must have been reflected in the throwing-out of old pieces of furniture and the acquiring of new. After all, they were, in Baker Street, in the very heart of London's Furniture Land. In Baker Street itself there was the well-known and still flourishing firm of Druce & Co, the widow of whose founder was the rather sinister heroine of one of the most extraordinary lawsuits of all time. She claimed that her dead husband, Thomas Charles Druce, had been, in reality, William John Cavendish-Bentinck-Scott, 5th Duke of Portland; or, to be more accurate, that, wishing to rid himself of his double existence as a London shopkeeper, the Duke had caused 'Druce' to 'die', burying what was, in truth, an empty coffin. This absurd and mischievous case went on for years, costing the 6th Duke of Portland much money to defend his patrimony, and rallying to Mrs Druce's side all the disaffected cranks in the kingdom, not the least vociferous being Robert Barr and Jerome K. Jerome, whose magazine, *The Idler,* constituted itself the champion of the claimant. The public subscribed heavily to limited companies formed to promote the claim and pay the share-holders back from 'the profits of the Portland Estate'. The case ran for over ten years; the public paying Mrs Druce's costs, and a handsome living into the bargain; the Duke of Portland, his own costs, which were heavy.

But, to return to furniture: a half-mile away was Tottenham Court Road which, with its continuation, Hampstead Road, had most of the new and old-established furniture shops in London: Oetzmann & Co, Schoolbred & Co and Maple & Co (still with us). Sir John Blundell Maple's daughter married the aristocratic Baron von Eckhardstein; they were married at Windsor, and the Baron did not wait until reaching London to declare himself—he blacked the newlywed Miss Maple's eyes in the train on the way from Windsor to London. In the same street were Woolf & Hollander (still flourishing), Davis (antiques and good reproductions, also still with us), and the interesting newcomer, Ambrose Heal, experimenting with the timid English Art Nouveau of Voisey, Frampton, Norman Shaw and, of course, Heal himself. Heal's is still in Tottenham Court Road, for the young Ambrose Heal, of the mottoed furniture vaguely reminiscent of Norwegian peasant art and vaguely reminiscent of lingering Pre-Raphaelitism, went on to become Sir Ambrose, an authority on old London tradesmen's cards (on which he wrote a book), and a father-figure of British furniture-making. His ghost haunts the existing premises in no uncertain manner.

So, with all these furniture shops offering bedroom-suites at anything from five guineas to fifteen hundred pounds, it seems to me impossible that Watson and Holmes did not, every now and then, re-furnish; or at least replace shabby old wickerwork tables, sagging, squeaky basket-chairs, and tatty cushions out of which the freshness had been sat over decades of bachelor existence. No, they must have smartened that room up: they didn't wish to move, they had got used to Mrs Hudson, the landlady-housekeeper, and the rent suited them; so they must have splurged a bit on new furnishings, if only to keep the page-in-buttons happy: servants do not understand loved shabbiness.

How Sir Henry Baskerville found the small hotel in the side-street off the then only ten-years-old Northumberland Avenue we are not told; perhaps Dr Mortimer, who had studied at, and walked the wards of, Charing Cross Hospital at-the-top-of-Northumberland-Street-and-cross-the-Strand might have found it for his titled friend. In any case, it had long been known to Holmes and Watson, who continued to be familiar with it long after Sir Henry Baskerville had come into the peaceful possession of his patrimony and his one real enemy was being mummified in the tannin of the Grimpen Mire. For in the little alley, Craven Passage, just outside the discreet back-door of that same 'Northumberland Arms' at which Sir Henry was putting up, was the ladies' entrance to the Holmes-and-Watson-patronised Charing Cross Turkish Baths—gentlemen's entrance, Northumberland Avenue. The premises are now a branch of Barclay's Bank, DCO, but the 'oriental' ladies' entrance may still be seen in Craven Passage, which was then called Northumberland Passage.

These Turkish baths were part of a then-flourishing chain of such establishments owned and run by Nevill's; all were open from 9.00 am to 7.00 pm at 3s 6d, and after 7.00 pm (all night, until 9.00 am on the following morning) at 2s. One could thus have a Turkish bath and a good night's sleep for a florin and whatever one tipped the attendant.

It was in the Charing Cross Turkish Baths, on Wednesday, 3 September 1902, that Holmes shewed Watson the letter received from Sir James Damery, and so began 'The Adventure of the Illustrious Client'— '. . . in some ways the supreme moment of my friend's career', says Watson.

Fourteen years had passed since Holmes had tidied up that sinister affair in Devonshire for the baronet who had stayed at the 'Northumberland Arms', but that Holmes and Watson continued to pass (and perhaps to use) it, is shown by the fact that, in 1902, we find them only a few yards away, in the hot-room of Nevill's.

NEVILL'S TURKISH BATHS

These baths stand on what was formerly part of the grounds of Northumberland House, occupied nearly three years in building, and involved an expenditure of £30,000. They comprise a suite of Bath Rooms, having a floor space of about twelve thousand square feet for gentlemen, with a smaller set in a separate contiguous building for the exclusive use of ladies. The cooling rooms, which are surmounted by a lofty dome designed to permit the free circulation of air and to ensure perfect ventilation, are fitted in a most luxurious manner; the whole of the decorations of both cooling and hot rooms have been designed by most eminent authorities; while the heating and ventilation of the hot chambers are brought to a state of perfection by the use of the system first introduced by the Proprietors.

Thus an advertisement of 1895. It does not seem to suffer from overwriting, and surely explains Watson's reasons for remarking that 'both Holmes and I had a weakness for the Turkish bath'. Now that the once popular Turkish bath has been displaced in popularity by the newer (newer to Britain, of course; not new to Finland) sauna bath, fewer people may appreciate the significance of Watson's remark: 'It was over a smoke in the pleasant lassitude of the drying-room that I have found him less reticent and more human than anywhere else'.

For all the rebuilding in this part of the world, the old atmosphere clings in an impressive manner; though now as shabby and forlorn as any building is on which the dead hand of government tenancy falls. The splendid hotels of 1880-1900 still line the western side of Northumberland Avenue; though now a BBC hall, the Playhouse still looks like a theatre, and along the tiny Craven Passage there is still one of the most remarkable survivals of eighteenth-century domestic architecture in London: Craven Street, in which both Heine and Benjamin Franklin lived, the latter when he was London agent for Pennsylvania. The well-preserved house in which he lived and worked is open to the public.

CHAPTER 10

A Look at Suburbia

Perhaps the greatest changes which have overtaken London during the decades since the end of World War II have occurred in the suburbs. The houses, many of them, are still there, and Sherlock Holmes would have no difficulty in recognising the general physical characteristics of, say, Norwood, Norbury, Anerley, Penge, Brixton, or of 'the Borough', that nearest of all suburbs just the other side of London Bridge. But he would miss the vast greyness of the Crystal Palace, thrusting its twin towers into what was sometimes—when the fog was clamped down on London—an even deeper grey.

The old houses of the south-east suburbs, in all the Victorian architectural styles from late classical to parsonage Gothic; from Osborne Italianate (seen at its best at Beckenham) to fussy neo-François Premier; can still be seen clothing the slopes of Norwood and Sydenham and Crystal Palace. But the former hotels and hydropathic establishments and City businessmen's villas have now been cut up into rooms or flats, with no one sufficiently interested, or sufficiently well-off, to care for the fabric, whose stucco, peeling and rotting over the unpainted years, lays bare the even more vulnerable core of these shabby buildings.

Holmes would wonder what had happened to the *people* of these once 'select' suburbs, where holystoned front steps, brightly polished front-door knobs and letter-slots, and crisply starched muslin blinds at the windows were the *sine qua non* of 'select' middle-class respectability. He would wonder at the blocks of flats; but not so much, or so despairingly, as at the decaying remains of the house-proud affluence that he and Watson knew when they went to Norbury in that disturbing 'Case of the Yellow Face'; to Upper Norwood, in April 1882; in that singular business of *The Sign of Four*; and to Norwood again in the matter of 'The Norwood Builder'. In the last-named case, the two friends went, you will recall, from London Bridge Station, which has been rebuilt since those now far-off days; it is newer, of course, but already the shabby look which overtakes all neglected modern buildings has begun to dim and rust the 'stainless' steel, smear and obscure windows and panels of coloured

'The George' inn, Southwark, last of London's many seventeenth-century galleried inns. In August 1895, when Holmes and Watson left from and returned to London Bridge Station, in the matter of 'The Norwood Builder' they may well have sought a little refreshment at 'The George' just around the corner from the station, then as now. Today, only the south side remains of the galleried quadrangle, which was intact when this picture was taken in 1895

glass, coat with grime and litter the unswept floors of station yard and 'concourse'.

Beyond London Bridge Station, under the railway bridge, the old look still clings: St Mary Overy, now the grander 'Southwark Cathedral', has been repaired since World War II's bombing; the still narrow Borough High Street, in which Mr Grant Munro pursued his (then important) business of hop-factor—all London's hop-factors were established in Borough High Street—retains many of the old buildings, including the remains of 'The George', London's last galleried inn, saved, God knows how, from total destruction at the hands of the 'cultured' but obviously money-before-everything directors of the London & North Eastern Railway, whose yard 'The George' had become nearly a century ago.

There are traces of the Marshalsea 'Debtors' prison up an alley off the High Street—Dickens's father was here imprisoned for debt—and the great breweries of Courage and Barclay, Perkins are still here, though the two firms merged some years ago. Commendably, they have improved some of their riverside pubs in the area, and 'The Anchor' and 'The Bankside' are well-furnished and lively places.

Holmes and Watson would feel at home in even modern Borough High Street, though most of the hop-factors have left. The 'London Bridge Tavern' has gone, and the bridge itself has been rebuilt and its stone facings sold to an American entrepreneur. But the wonderful old Charles II houses in St Thomas's Street are not only standing, having survived both World Wars, but are now well looked after. And though there has been some shoddy and unimaginative additions to Guy's Hospital, around the corner, the noble main building has been permitted to survive. Watson, at least, would have missed that!

The greatest changes in the suburbs have come through the disappearance of a suburban class: professional and semi-professional, upper trading and the senior grades of civil servant. Many of these had attained, as their surviving, divided-up, houses plainly show, the rank of 'carriage folk'. Consumed by a restless ambition to 'better themselves'—the paradox is more apparent than real—they were yet content to establish themselves in as permanent a situation as possible, and to be content in having risen to the stratum they had attained. Well-dressed and living in houses kept, inside and out, in spotless condition by well-trained and generally well-contented servants, these were the people whose modest but unceasing achievements made up the real wealth of a world-leading Britain. When the suburban buttresses of national wealth and national pride were taxed, persecuted or simply neglected out of existence, national wealth and pride vanished, too.

Holmes would not have been too surprised to see the overhead telephone and electric light cables—so thick in any picture of London (especially of the City) taken between 1880 and 1920—go underground. Nor would he have regretted, too much, the vanishing of those old houses, in Cornhill, Old Jewry, Aldgate, Leadenhall Street and many other places, which gave the City the air of an eighteenth century quarter into which a few Victorian buildings had accidentally strayed. Holmes cared little one feels, for the past. One remembers his enthusiasm as he gazed out of the train at the Board Schools of Clapham Junction (there are three to be seen from the train as it goes through the Junction). 'Lighthouses of the future'! he exulted, as he pointed out the school or schools to Watson.

Clapham, like any other suburb, has lost the suburban house-pride which gave its terraces of tiny villas the air of a garden city, despite the smoke from station and an occasional factory. To-day it is terrifying in its squalid decay, the new Greater London Council blocks of flats adding to, rather than detracting from, its despairing ugliness.

The fine school buildings of the now vanished London School Board rise indeed like lighthouses over the disintegrating houses of Clapham: a source of irritation to those 'developers' who have a vested interest in putting something—anything—in the place of something else; money to pull down the old, money to put up the fragile, temporary and soul-less new.

They were coming up to London proper when Holmes made that remark about lighthouses; all sensible people will continue the journey to London. In the capital, at least, though there is organised destruction, especially of anything which recalls too pointedly the rich, proud, self-respecting past, there is still survival. Quite a lot, indeed, to link the London of to-day's empire-less Britain with the rich, comfortable, self-assured London of Sherlock Holmes.

It is not the bustle and the go-getting, the energy, for good or ill, the up-and-doing restlessness which link the vanished world of Holmes with our own. All ages have known their individual types of energy, their peculiar ambitions. Rather are we linked with Holmes and many earlier ages, not by how we strive but by how we seek—and find—peace for contemplation; a quiet place in all the frantic striving. London has always had such quiet places, and it is these which link our modern London most strongly with the past. Within the soaring arches of Westminster Abbey or, under God's sky, in the incredible peace of the Abbey's cloistered garden, we may seek and always find those restful backwaters of the physical and the spiritual that London has always had to offer to both its citizens and the most transient of its visitors

BIBLIOGRAPHY

The bibliography of Sherlock Holmes is immense: there is no other word for it. As Ellery Queen said in the introduction to his suppressed anthology, *The Misadventure of Sherlock Holmes* (1944): 'Someone has said that more has been written *about* Sherlock Holmes than about any other character in fiction. It is further true that more has been written about Holmes *by others* than by Doyle himself'. As there is not even the permissible author's exaggeration in this remark by one of the world's greatest detective-story writers, it is clear that it would be impossible to list even a thousandth of what has been written—articles and books—on the perennially fascinating subject of Sherlock Holmes. What I list below are the *main* sources of information on the two linked subjects of this book: the London of Holmes's day and, of course, Holmes himself.

The files of London newspapers, surviving and defunct, have yielded much information, as well as those illustrated journals which, in the days before the 'telly', provided the eagerly sought pictorial comment on the news: such journals as *The Queen, The Graphic, The Sphere, The Illustrated London News, Country Sport, The Field, Madame, London Letter, The King, Black & White,* and—at a lower but still successful end of the scale—*The Penny Illustrated Newspaper* and *The Police Gazette* (both invaluable for the student of Victorian crime).

Only principal sources are listed; works which have merely yielded a casual reference are not quoted, though they are, of course, mentioned in the text.

Anonymous. *Fifty Years of London Society*
Baring-Gould, W. S. *Sherlock Holmes of Baker Street, A Life of the World's First Consulting Detective*
—— *The Annotated Sherlock Holmes*
Bell, W. G. *Unknown London*
Brend, Gavin. *My Dear Holmes: a Study in Sherlock*
Blakeney, T. S. *Sherlock Holmes: Fact or Fiction?*
Christ, Jay Finley. *An Irregular Guide to Sherlock Holmes*
Clunn, Harold P. *The Face of London*
Collins's Illustrated Guide to London (1883)

Cook, Mrs E. T. *Highways and Byways in London*
Davis, Lt Col R. Newnham. *Diners and Dining Out*
—— *The Gourmet's Guide to London*
Gomme, Sir Laurence. *London in the Reign of Victoria, 1837-1897*
Handbook to London As It Is (1879). Anon.; published by John
　Murray
Hall, Trevor H. *Sherlock Holmes*
Harben, FSA, Henry A. *A Dictionary of London*
Harper, Charles G. *A Londoner's Own London, 1870-1920*
Harrison, Michael. *In the Footsteps of Sherlock Holmes*
—— *London Beneath the Pavement*
—— *London by Gaslight*
—— *London Growing*
Haydn's Dictionary of Dates
Holden, W. H. *They Startled Grandfather—Gay Ladies and Merry
　Mashers of Victorian Times*
Holroyd, James E. (Editor). *Seventeen Steps to 221B Baker Street
　Byways*
Laver, James. *Victorian Panorama*
Loftie, Rev W. J. *In and Out of London*
London: A Complete Guide (1876). Anon. Published by Henry
　Herbert & Co
Morris, O. *Grandfather's London*
Nevill, Lady Dorothy. *Under Five Reigns*
Nevill, Ralph. *The Life and Letters of Lady Dorothy Nevill* (ed.
　Ralph Nevill)
'One of the Old Boys'. *London in the Sixties*
'One of Her Majesty's Servants'. *The Private Life of the Queen* (ie,
　Victoria)
Osgood Field, Julian (published as 'Anonymous'). *Things I shouldn't
　Tell*
—— *Uncensored Recollections*
—— *More Uncensored Recollections*
Pascoe's Guide to London
Post Office Directory (London)
'Resident, A Foreign'. *Society in London*
—— *Society in the New Reign* (ie, of Edward VII)
Sala, George Augustus. *Twice Around the Clock*
Thornbury, G. W. (*see* Walford, E.)

Wagner, Leopold. *A New Book About London—A Quaint and Curious Volume of Forgotten Lore*

Walford, E. ('Thornbury'). *Old and New London*

Warrack, Guy. *Sherlock Holmes and Music*

Wheatley, Henry B. *London Past and Present; Its History, Association and Traditions*

Whitaker's Almanack

Wright, Jessie D. *London's Old Buildings*

Zeisler, Ernest B. *Baker Street Chronology: Commentaries on the Sacred Writings of Dr John H. Watson*

The Sherlockian periodical press is extensive and must, of course, be treated separately. In addition to the scholarly yet eminently readable, and always well-produced journals of the two principal Sherlockian societies, the Baker Street Irregulars (New York) and the Sherlock Holmes Society of London—respectively *The Baker Street Journal* (editor, Julian Woolf, MD) and *The Sherlock Holmes Journal* (editor, the Marquess of Donegall)—there are the many journals, some of them only mimeographed, produced by and for the various 'scion societies' now established in all the five continents. Where publication is irregular and production still amateurish, one feels confident that extended circulation and growing financial resources will eventually bring the majority of these 'scion' journals up to the standard now established by Lord Donegall and Dr Wolff.

It would be invidious to make comparisons, but I may single out two of these 'subsidiary' (perhaps 'independent' is the fairer word) journals for honourable mention: *The Baker Street Gasogene* (New York), a commendable quarterly edited by P. A. Ruber, and *Sherlockiana*, a magazine in which the 'digest' principle is still dominant. The latter, now edited by the well-known artist, Henry Lauritzen (and before that by A. D. Henriksen), is the journal of the Sherlock Holmes Klubben i Danmark ('The Danish Baker Street Irregulars'). To the dedicated student of Sherlockismus, the comments and criticisms of this imposing output of periodical literature is, as they say, a 'must'.

Let me end with the words of Dr Watson in *The Hound of the Baskervilles*: 'Has anything escaped me? . . . I trust there is nothing of consequence which I have overlooked'.

ACKNOWLEDGEMENTS

After one or two books—and I have now written over fifty—an author's research tends to reveal a marked pattern, from which he or she does not, and would not, stray. Research, from book to book, alters only in the identity of the sources of information, not in their general nature.

I have already indicated in the Bibliography the principal sources consulted; what I did not mention there were the means by which I was helpfully put in touch with those sources.

Once again, the three principal Westminster City Council libraries—the Central Reference, in St Martin's Street; the Buckingham Palace Road branch (with its unrivalled Westminster Collection of archives, both literary and pictorial); the former Marylebone Public Library, in Marylebone Road (with its rich Sherlockian archives)—have afforded me much valuable information, their always helpful and informed staff as willing as ever to assist a researching author.

The staffs of the Photographic Library of the British Tourist Authority, London Transport and the Department of Medical Illustration, St Bartholomew's Hospital, well deserve my thanks, as does the Public Relations Department at New Scotland Yard, not only for having supplied me with three excellent illustrations, but also for having obtained for me the permission of the Commissioner of Police of the Metropolis to use them in this book.

Sherlockians all over the world, as well as non-Sherlockian inhabitants of Baker Street and its environs, have made many useful suggestions: alas, these helpers are too numerous to be mentioned by name here. My sincere thanks to them all.

Special thanks go to the directors of Haslemere Estates Ltd for the fine photograph of 109 Baker Street, reproduced on page 42; and to Mr Tony Mann, for having so carefully and successfully recorded for me the appearance of 24 Montague Street before (in all probability) it suffers the fate now threatened.

I should also like to say a word here about the support that I received in the middle of 1971 from the directors of Williams & Glyn's Bank Ltd; support which, though not *directly* connected with this book, brought me in touch with many a fruitful idea herein embodied.

On my announcing that a revised a re-illustrated version of my *In the*

221

Footsteps of Sherlock Holmes was then due shortly to appear, the directors of the Bank generously offered to mount an exhibition of Sherlockian material (most of it from my own collection) in a fully professional manner in the hall of the Bank's premises at 101/3 Baker Street. This most successful exhibition, originally intended to last a week, was extended a further week in response to obvious public demand: the first time, in the world's history, I understand, that a Bank has mounted an exhibition to further a customer's work.

I mention this generous gesture of the Bank's to indicate that it is not always in the more *expected* ways that an author—especially if he or she be a researcher—gets his inspiration and information. What the exhibition at Williams & Glyn's Bank did was to bring much information to me, rather than (in the ordinary way) that I went out to seek it.

My American and other foreign friends of Sherlockian bent gave me encouragement and helpful ideas: in particular, Luther Norris of Culver City ('Lord Warden of the Pontine Marshes'), Frederic Dannay (surviving partner of 'Ellery Queen') and Herr A. D. Henriksen, for many years Editor of *Sherlockiana* and still Director-general of the Danish Baker Street Irregulars. Thanks, too, to my old friend and fellow-worker in the fields of Sherlockian research, Edward Holroyd, for reminding me of wha I had said in my *In the Footsteps of Sherlock Holmes*.

INDEX

Bold type indicates that the subject is depicted.   Abbreviations: c =caption;
n =footnote

223